RIVAL SISTERS

Mary & Elizabeth Tudor

Copyright © Sylvia Barbara Soberton 2019

The right of Sylvia Barbara Soberton to be identified as the Author of the Work has been asserted by her in accordance with the Copyright, Designs and Patents Act 1988.

All rights reserved. No part of this publication may be reproduced, stored in a retrieval system, or transmitted, in any form or by any means }uiwithout the prior written permission of the publisher, nor be otherwise circulated in any form of binding or cover other than in which it is published and without a similar condition being imposed on the subsequent purchaser.

Facebook page:
www.facebook.com/theforgottentudorwomen

Twitter:
https://twitter.com/SylviaBSo

Editorial services: Jennifer Quinlan
http://historicaleditorial.blogspot.com/

ISBN: 9781701605350

This book is dedicated to my daughter, Amanda, who makes me proud every day.

Contents

Prologue: Together for eternity 1

Chapter 1: "The Little Bastard" 4

Chapter 2: "No other Queen than my mother" 15

Chapter 3: "As long as that woman lived" 25

Chapter 4: "Concerning the Princess" 47

Chapter 5: "Your loving sister, Elizabeth" 69

Chapter 6: "Completely reconciled" 77

Chapter 7: "My sister was so incensed against me" 112

Chapter 8: "Your truth" 133

Chapter 9: "Anatomies of hearts" 170

Chapter 10: "She hates the Queen" 188

Epilogue: Elizabeth after Mary 206

Picture section 239

Selected Bibliography 249

Prologue:
Together for Eternity

Mary and Elizabeth, the Tudor half sisters who became the first two English Queens regnant respectively, lie buried together in one vault in the North Aisle of Henry VII's Lady Chapel in Westminster Abbey. A commemorative Latin plaque at the head of the monument reads: "Partners both in throne and grave, here rest we two sisters Elizabeth and Mary, in the hope of one resurrection."[1]

According to the official guide to Westminster Abbey, Mary's coffin lies beneath Elizabeth's. But neither Elizabeth, who died in 1603, nor Mary, who predeceased her by forty-five years, chose to be buried in this way. Mary died on 17 November 1558 at St James's Palace and was buried according to Catholic rites in an unmarked grave on the North Aisle of the Lady Chapel. Mary never made a tomb for herself during her lifetime, but in her last will she requested that she be buried next to her mother, Katharine of Aragon, whose remains she willed to be transferred from Peterborough to Westminster. This was never done. As her half sister's successor, Elizabeth was expected to provide an honourable burial and honour Mary's dying wish, but she failed to memorialise her. "The stones from . . . broken altars were piled upon Mary's grave during the whole of her sister's reign."²

Elizabeth died on 24 March 1603 at Richmond Palace after forty-five years on the throne. Unmarried and childless, she designated James VI of Scotland, the son of her executed rival Mary Stuart, as her successor. England's Virgin Queen was buried in the crypt beneath the altar, in the Sepulchre of her grandfather, Henry VII. Three years later Elizabeth's coffin was placed on top of that of her half sister. King James made sure that a gilded effigy of Elizabeth decorated the newly erected tomb, but there was no effigy of Mary, the only acknowledgement of her presence there being the Latin inscription.

Burying the childless Elizabeth with her half sister served King James's purpose of emphasising that "virgins do not found or further the greatness of dynasties".³ A larger and grander tomb was built at Westminster Abbey for James's mother, Mary Stuart, Queen of Scots, who was executed on Elizabeth's orders in 1587 and was originally buried at Peterborough Cathedral. In life, James had no warm feelings for the woman who gave birth to him, but he honoured her in death to celebrate the royal lineage he was born into.

It is the relationship between Elizabeth and her Scottish cousin Mary Stuart that is often discussed and pondered over while the relationship between Elizabeth and her own half sister is largely forgotten. Yet it is the relationship with Mary Tudor that forged Elizabeth's personality and set her on the path to queenship. Mary's reign was the darkest period in Elizabeth's life. "I stood in danger of my life, my sister was so incensed against me", Elizabeth reminded her councillors when they pressed her to name a successor.[4] Elizabeth harboured resentment against Mary even after the latter's death, but she refrained from speaking ill of her. Even if the cause of her ill treatment was Mary, Elizabeth sighed, "I will not now burden her therewith because I will not charge the dead".[5]

It is time to tell the whole story of the fierce rivalry between the Tudor half sisters who became their father's successors.

NOTES

[1] *Regno consortes et urna, hic obdor mimus Elizabetha et Maria sorores, in spe resurrectionis.*
[2] Julia M. Walker, *Reading the Tombs of Elizabeth I*, p. 522.
[3] Ibid., p. 524.
[4] Clark Hulse, *Elizabeth I: Ruler and Legend*, p. 26.
[5] John Nichols, *The Progresses and Public Processions of Queen Elizabeth*, Volume 1, p. 64.

Chapter 1:
"The Little Bastard"

On 7 September 1533, Henry VIII's second wife—"that famous Anne Boleyn", as she was to be remembered twenty years later—gave birth to her first and only child.[1] The King's astrologers and soothsayers predicted the birth of a long-awaited male heir, and Henry expected Anne to make good on her promise. During their courtship, she had inserted a loving couplet under a miniature of the Annunciation, the angel Gabriel telling the Virgin Mary that she would have a son: "By daily proof you shall me find to be to you both loving and kind." Whether it was a deliberate enticement or just an innocent allusion to the expected reaping of the fruits of marriage, the King took it literally and hoped that Anne would give him a son. When the imperial ambassador Eustace Chapuys somewhat sardonically reminded the King that a new wife was by no means a guarantee of male heirs, Henry VIII exploded in anger, asking: "Am I not a man like others?"[2] Other men Henry knew had sons, whereas he had only one legitimate daughter and a bastard son who could not inherit his throne. The King was desperate to sire a male heir and prove his virility to the world.

This obsession with the outcome of Anne Boleyn's pregnancy was a culmination of events set in motion by Henry VIII in 1527. After eighteen years of marriage to the Spanish Katharine of Aragon, Henry VIII had no male heirs to show for it. Sons came and went, some dying instantly after birth, others living beyond delivery only to be snatched away by cruel death within days or months. Katharine of Aragon took her infants' deaths as God's will, but Henry VIII saw them as God's wrath. "If a man marries his brother's widow, they shall be childless", warned the biblical Book of Leviticus.

By 1527, Henry had convinced himself that he had committed a sin by marrying his late brother's widow. Katharine of Aragon claimed that her marriage to Prince Arthur was never consummated and thus was invalid according to church law, but her husband had other ideas. He had convinced himself that by marrying Katharine he had incurred God's wrath, and although they had a living child together, Mary, the King believed that if his mistress (Bessie Blount) was able to bear him a son, so any other woman—except his Queen—would be able to do so.

Some people believed that there were other, more sinister reasons behind the King's wish to repudiate his wife. Anne Boleyn, "a fresh young damsel" who had returned from the French court in 1521, had caught Henry VIII's attention. After almost seven years spent at the glittering French court, Anne was regarded as a Frenchwoman in her appearance, style and manners. The King, who was dazzled by all things French, from clothes to the hairstyle he wore, was instantly smitten. Anne possessed every quality the King valued in a woman. She was well educated, elegant and well versed in the art of courtly love. She could speak French fluently, sing and dance and accompany herself on the lute and clavichord. As the sister of a poet, she also had a deep appreciation of literature.

The King's mistress who had borne him a son, Bessie Blount, was said to excel in singing, dancing and other courtly pastimes, but Anne, although inferior to her in beauty, excelled all other women at court with her grace and winning manner. Her trump card was her European education. No other Englishwoman had that aura of Continental gloss about her, and Anne quickly became one of the brightest stars of Henry VIII's court.

No wonder, then, that the King desired to add her name to the ever-expanding list of his royal mistresses. But Anne was not interested in becoming yet another mistress of the King of England, like her sister before her, and refused to countenance the idea. What made her refusal so dangerous was that it coincided with Henry VIII's doubts about the validity of his marriage to Katharine of Aragon. The King had pondered repudiating Katharine in 1514, but the idea was dropped, and two years later, on 18 February 1516, the Queen gave birth to a healthy daughter, Princess Mary. Henry consoled himself that both he and Katharine were still young and thus able to have sons, but no son was born, and by 1527 Henry had given up hope.

Anne's refusal was also dangerous because she had a taste for reform, which she had acquired while in France. Historians often put Anne's decision down to cold ambition, but the surviving evidence points to the fact that she abhorred the idea of losing her good name. In an epistle penned to her father when she was a teenager, Anne mused: "I understand from your letter that you desire me to be a woman of good reputation when I come to court."[3] The strong desire to please her father coupled with her religious devotion may well have been deciding factors in refusing Henry VIII's advances.

Ideas "injurious to the pope" were "frequently instilled" in Henry VIII's mind, wrote Cardinal Thomas Wolsey, who recognised Anne Boleyn's influence on the enamoured King.[4] It was Anne who gave Henry her own copy of a banned book entitled *The Obedience of a Christian Man*, wherein William Tyndale argued that popes had no authority over kings. Later in her life she took credit for extricating the King "from a state of sin", meaning his first marriage and membership in the Church of Rome.[5]

Katharine of Aragon hoped that once Anne Boleyn's intoxicating charm wore off, the King would come to his senses and abandon the divorce proceedings. But with each passing year, Henry VIII's fascination with Anne grew proportionally to his anger at the pope, who steadfastly refused to agree to his terms and give him his longed-for annulment. Observing Henry VIII's growing infatuation, the Queen acknowledged that Anne Boleyn was not a mere passing fancy and berated her husband for setting a scandalous example by keeping his mistress lodged at court "without the least particle of shame".[6] To Henry, his wife's argument was invalid. His relationship with Anne was pure because it was not carnal, and he kept her close because he wanted to learn her character before they married. Anne knew that the Queen always had the upper hand during arguments and reproached Henry for engaging in heated disputes with her. "I see that some fine morning you will succumb to her reasoning and cast me off", she bitterly complained.[7] It was a grudging compliment to the Queen's tenacity and intellect.

As the years went on, Henry VIII's annulment reached a stalemate, and Anne complained that her childbearing years were running out. "I have been waiting long and might in the meanwhile have contracted some advantageous marriage, out of which I might have had issue, which is the greatest consolation in this world", she complained. "But alas, farewell to my time and youth spent to no purpose at all", she added with a touch of pathos.[8]

By late 1532, Anne had everything except the crown and the baby she so desperately wanted. The King invested her with the noble title of Marchioness of Pembroke, worth £1,000 per year, gave her a semi-regal residence at Hanworth and adorned her person with Katharine of Aragon's jewels. On their way from the meeting with Francis I of France in Calais in the autumn of 1532, Henry and Anne exchanged solemn vows and consummated their relationship. Within weeks Anne discovered she was pregnant, and the King married her during a clandestine ceremony in the upper chamber over the Holbein Gate at Whitehall Palace on 25 January 1533. Anne's path to her coronation at Westminster Abbey went straight from there. She was crowned on 1 June 1533, and two months later she withdrew from public life at court in anticipation of the birth of her son.

Just like Katharine of Aragon before her, the new Queen claimed a chamber inside Greenwich Palace for her lying in. Anne must have either miscalculated or her baby was premature because she went into labour only twelve days after entering her confinement. According to the imperial ambassador Chapuys, the sight of the infant daughter caused "great regret" to both Henry and Anne, but they brazened it out and organised a lavish christening.[9] Because the child was born on the eve of the Virgin's Nativity, Chapuys erroneously assumed that the King's new child would be named Mary, like Henry's elder daughter. The baby girl was christened Elizabeth, like both of her grandmothers, and received the title of Princess of England.

Within days of Elizabeth's birth, Henry VIII sent new instructions to Sir John Hussey, chamberlain in the household of his elder daughter, Mary. Hussey communicated to Mary that "her high estate of the name and dignity of Princess" would be diminished. Mary was speechless. Groomed to become her father's successor from an early age, she could not understand why she was now declared to be the mere "Lady Mary, the King's illegitimate daughter".[10] But it was the reality of Mary's life now. Her mother, Katharine of Aragon, was no longer Queen of England, but Princess Dowager of Wales, and her marriage to Henry VIII was declared null and void. The King now wanted to emphasise that his only lawfully married wife was Anne Boleyn, and their daughter, Elizabeth, was his successor. The King wanted the change of Mary's status to be reflected in her new living arrangements and placed her in Elizabeth's newly established household.

On 13 December 1533, Elizabeth, the new Princess of Wales, was ceremoniously escorted to her household at Hatfield accompanied by a train of dukes, earls and lords. The next day Thomas Howard, Duke of Norfolk, arrived at Mary's residence at the Palace of Beaulieu and presented her with the King's summons to enter the service of her younger half sister. Norfolk called Elizabeth the Princess of Wales, but Mary defiantly informed the duke that "this title belonged to herself and to no other".[11] Norfolk listened patiently as Mary poured her soul out to him, but he said he was not there to dispute with her, but to accomplish his mission. Seeing Norfolk's indifference, Mary went to her private apartments to copy the protestation sent to her by the imperial ambassador:

"My Lords, as touching my removal to Hatfield, I will obey his Grace, as my duty is, or to any place his Grace will appoint me. But I protest before you and all others that be here present, that my conscience will in no wise suffer me to take any other than myself for the King's lawful daughter, born in true matrimony, or princess; and that I will never willingly and wittingly say or do, whereby any person might take occasion to think that I agree to the contrary."[12]

Mary journeyed from Beaulieu to Hatfield with only two servants in attendance. When she was showed her new chambers, she discovered that they were not as lavishly decorated as those at Beaulieu, but she appeared undeterred. When Norfolk invited Mary to pay her respects to Princess Elizabeth, she replied that she knew no other princess except herself and that "the Marchioness of Pembroke's daughter held no such title".[13] She added that since the King acknowledged Elizabeth as his daughter, she might call her sister, just like she called Henry Fitzroy her brother, but she insisted she could do no more. With this one sentence, Mary made it luminously clear that she could not accept that her mother had been replaced as Queen by Anne Boleyn, whom she called Marchioness of Pembroke as if she were oblivious to the fact that Anne was crowned and anointed just as her own mother had been twenty-four years earlier.

In reality, Henry VIII had two crowned queens on one island, and many people sneered at Anne's elevation, calling her a "goggle-eyed whore" and a "harlot". Since Anne was not the Queen in Mary's view, Elizabeth was not a royal princess. The imperial ambassador invented a malicious nickname for Elizabeth in his dispatches—"the Little Bastard"—and it's clear that Mary shared his sentiment. Mary came to perceive the cooing infant sleeping in a cradle of estate as a living embodiment of Henry VIII's betrayal of her and her mother. But rather than blaming her royal father for the dramatic change in her circumstances, Mary chose to lay the blame squarely at the feet of Elizabeth's mother, Anne Boleyn.

NOTES

[1] *Calendar of State Papers, Venice,* Volume 6, n. 884.
[2] *Calendar of State Papers, Spain,* Volume 4 Part 2, n. 1061.
[3] Eric Ives, *The Life and Death of Anne Boleyn,* p. 20.
[4] *Letters and Papers, Henry VIII,* Volume 4, n. 4897.
[5] Ibid., Volume 8, n. 666.
[6] Paul Friedmann, *Anne Boleyn,* Volume 1, p. 130.
  Calendar of State Papers, Spain, Volume 4 Part 2, n. 681.
[7] *Letters and Papers, Henry VIII,* Volume 4 Part 1, n. 224.
[8] Ibid.
[9] *Letters and Papers, Henry VIII,* Volume 6, n. 1112.

[10] Ibid., n. 1139.
[11] Ibid., n. 1528.
[12] Peter Heylyn, *Ecclesia Restaurata*, Volume 2, p. 70.
[13] *Letters and Papers, Henry VIII,* Volume 6, 1533, n. 1558.

Chapter 2: "No other Queen than my mother"

In early 1534, both Mary's and Elizabeth's circumstances changed dramatically. In March, the pope proclaimed that Henry VIII's marriage to Katharine of Aragon was lawful, but the King did not care anymore. As far as he was concerned, Katharine was not his wife since Thomas Cranmer, Archbishop of Canterbury, had proclaimed their marriage invalid in May 1533. Also in March 1534, Henry VIII's acquiescent Parliament passed the new Act of Succession, investing children born to Henry and Anne Boleyn as the King's heirs. Mary was thus barred from inheriting the crown and replaced by Elizabeth and any other child born to Anne Boleyn.

Mary and her mother clung desperately to the pope's decision, which came nearly five years after Katharine of Aragon appealed to Rome, and remained unmoved in their decision to oppose the King. Mary had not seen her mother since Katharine of Aragon was banished from court in 1531. Mother and daughter were, however, allowed to exchange letters. At some point after Mary's degradation from a position of honour, Katharine wrote a long epistle wherein she urged Mary to obey "the King your father in everything, save that you will not offend God and lose your own soul". Katharine must have heard rumours that Henry VIII and Anne Boleyn were planning to marry Mary beneath her station because she urged her "to keep your heart with a chaste mind, and your body from all ill and wanton company, not thinking or desiring any husband for Christ's passion". She encouraged Mary to stand her ground because "we never come to the kingdom of Heaven but by troubles".[1]

Mary's formative years were marked by much sorrow and insecurity. Not only was she pained by the separation from her mother, but she also had to come to terms with her father's cold indifference towards her. The King kept Mary at a physical and emotional distance. He removed her trusted servants, such as Margaret Pole, the elderly Countess of Salisbury, replacing her with Anne Shelton, the paternal aunt of Anne Boleyn. Mary did not expect her new Lady Mistress to treat her with warm feelings because Lady Shelton's loyalty lay with Queen Anne, but even Shelton found her imperious niece's instructions to be too harsh. Whenever Mary used the title of "princess," Anne Shelton was to "box her ears and slap her face as a cursed bastard that she was". Mary also had a habit of eating large breakfasts in her chamber, but Anne Boleyn now ordered that Mary was to be starved back into the great hall, where she would eat with other members of the household. Lady Shelton could hardly act upon these instructions, and she treated Mary with "too great kindness and regard", for which she was rebuffed by Anne Boleyn's brother and uncle. With a dose of defiance, Shelton replied that even if Mary "was the bastard daughter of a poor gentleman, her kindness, her modesty and her virtues called forth all respect and honour". And because Mary was the King's daughter, Anne Shelton was determined to treat her as such.[2]

Understandably, Mary chose to see her father as a victim of his manipulative new wife. She naively believed that it was Anne who kept the King away from her, and she decided to defy both Anne and her daughter, Elizabeth. Such a view was simplistic, but it allowed Mary, caught between her estranged parents and a hostile stepmother, to find a culprit other than her father, who she believed loved her still. This may have been true as Chapuys reported that Anne hated Mary "as much as" she loathed Katharine of Aragon or even "more so, chiefly because she sees the King has some affection for her". During her rise to power, Anne made no attempt to befriend the King's daughter, and it was rumoured that Henry never invited Mary to court to gratify Anne's wish. Whenever he visited her, Anne sent her women to spy on them. It appears that Anne saw both Katharine of Aragon and Mary as her rivals. On one occasion, when the King praised Mary in her presence, Anne "began to vituperate the Princess very strangely".[3] She didn't regard Mary as a person, but rather as a symbol of the King's first marriage. She even took it upon herself to plan Mary's marriage, hoping to marry her to her first cousin, the Earl of Surrey. Such a marriage would effectively put Mary out of the international marriage market, where she was regarded as heiress to the English throne. For his part, Henry VIII used Mary as a bargaining chip in his dealings with Katharine of Aragon. When an Act of Parliament forbade Katharine to use the title of Queen, it also stipulated that if she failed to accept her new position as the Dowager Princess of Wales, the King would be compelled to withdraw his affection from Mary. But Katharine never succumbed to Henry's threats because she firmly believed that he loved Mary and would never hurt her. For her part, Katharine always emphasised that she valued her marriage and status as Queen more than she valued her relationship with her daughter. She saw her divine calling of being a queen as more sacred than that of being a mother. Mary was not only her child, she was her heiress and a granddaughter of Isabella of Castile, who ruled in Spain in her own right. Mary was thus not only Katharine's child but a vessel of her hopes for the future, her royal descendant who would carry her legacy into the next generation and beyond. Once, when Katharine asked the King if Mary could visit them at court, the King "rebuffed her very rudely" and told her that she might visit Mary and stay with her if she so wished. Katharine's reply encapsulated her thoughts about her marriage, queenship and motherhood: "Neither for the sake of her own daughter, nor for any other person in the world would she consent to anything that would look like a separation from her husband."[4]

Anne Boleyn's hatred for Katharine of Aragon was legendary. On one occasion in 1531, she defiantly declared to one of Katharine's ladies-in-waiting that she would rather see Katharine hanged than ever acknowledge that she was her superior. On the other hand, Anne displayed insecurity over her status when she demanded that Katharine send her the "rich baptismal robe" she had brought from Spain in 1501 for the christening of her own child. Needless to say, Katharine staunchly refused. Over the course of the divorce proceedings, she never deigned to refer to Anne by name, but variously described her rival as "the woman he [Henry VIII] has under his roof" or "the companion the King now takes everywhere with him".[5] The most derogatory remark Katharine made about Anne was "the scandal of Christendom, and a disgrace to the King".[6]

When a delegation of privy councillors visited Katharine in July 1533, she defiantly informed them that she would never acknowledge Henry's "clandestine and accursed marriage" to Anne. From such an "abominable marriage there could only arise a perverse offspring", she retorted, "who would throw the kingdom into confusion if allowed to reign".[7] These were strong words from a woman who was not about to back down. She fought not only for her husband and royal title, but, above all, for her daughter's right to succeed to the throne. Anne and her child mattered little to Katharine, and there is no doubt that her hatred for Anne was as strong as Anne's for her.

When Anne visited her infant daughter at Eltham Palace early in 1534, she sent Mary a message wherein she urged her to come to her presence and acknowledge her as Queen. If Mary did so, the message said, Anne would act as an intermediary between Mary and the King and try to reconcile them. Mary answered with a great deal of insolence:

"I know no other Queen in England than my mother, but if the King's mistress would do me the favour she spoke of and intercede with the King, my father, I would certainly be most grateful."[8]

Anne Boleyn was not put off by this rebuff and repeated her "profuse offers" but departed threatening to "bring down the pride of this unbridled Spanish blood".[9] Whereas Mary chose to perceive Anne as the villain, it is clear that it was Henry VIII who made all decisions touching his daughter. He saw Mary as a disobedient and unruly child who chose to side with her mother. This was unacceptable to the King, who believed that children's obedience should be primarily to their fathers. He was aware that until he had a son Mary would keep defying him. When the imperial ambassador Chapuys boldly told the King that it was Mary's hereditary right to succeed before her younger half sister, the King replied that "there was no other princess except his daughter Elizabeth, until he had a son which he thought would happen soon".[10] Henry was alluding to Anne Boleyn's second pregnancy, which had been public knowledge since January 1534.

Mary's hatred towards Anne Boleyn was incited by the imperial ambassador Chapuys, who kept her informed about goings-on at court. Chapuys himself was strongly biased against Anne, whose evangelical views and pro-French political sympathies disgusted him. The ambassador's informants belonged to the conservative faction at court. Among them were people like the cunning Gertrude Courtenay, Marchioness of Exeter, who was strongly devoted to Katharine of Aragon and Mary. She was no friend of Anne's since Anne had removed Gertrude from Katharine's service in 1530. As "the sole consolation" of Katharine and Mary, Gertrude despised Anne. She and her husband remained in close contact with Margaret Pole and her sons and often debated the political situation at court. The Poles and Courtenays believed that the King decided to divorce their "good Queen Katharine" because he was "in the snare of unlawful love with the lady Anne" and mocked the reformed Church of England, seeing it as a by-product of Henry's infatuation with Anne.[11] Anne, who was elevated to peerage and queenly honour due to Henry VIII's favour, was disparaged as "a harlot and a heretic"; she represented everything the conservative courtiers hated the most.[12]

Gertrude Courtenay and her husband often communicated with Chapuys and tried to convince him that

Anne was dangerous because she desired to put Katharine of Aragon and Mary to death. The threats were especially meaningful in the summer of 1534 when the pregnant Anne expected to be made regent if the King went to the meeting with Francis I in Calais. She boasted that she could poison Mary or starve her to death "even if she were burnt alive for it". Mary knew about Anne's boasts and told Chapuys she would be happy to gain paradise if she were to die poisoned by her father's despised concubine. Encouraged by Chapuys, she refused to accept the offers of Anne's father and William Paulet, who visited her on 13 July 1534, trying to convince her "to renounce her title, in which case the King would treat her better than she could wish, but if she refused it would be quite the contrary".[13]

Yet despite her outward bravado, each time Mary was visited by her father's commissioners, she was weaker. During the summer of 1534, she could hardly withstand the psychological pressure, and her health deteriorated dramatically. "The Princess has been very ill", Chapuys wrote on 27 September 1534. He believed she fell ill because she was obliged to remove from her lodgings "and follow the Bastard when a little indisposed". Mary's condition was so serious that the King sent his own physician to treat her and allowed Katharine of Aragon to come and see her; this is often overlooked by historians who state that Katharine and Mary never met after 1531.[14] This sudden change in Henry VIII's treatment of Mary reflects his love for his elder daughter and, perhaps, a personal disappointment. That summer, Anne Boleyn was not by Henry's side. She had given birth to a stillborn child, dashing the King's hopes for a male heir yet again.

NOTES

[1] *Letters and Papers, Foreign and Domestic, Henry VIII,* Volume 6, n. 1126.
[2] Sylvia Barbara Soberton, *Great Ladies,* pp. 70-71.
[3] *Letters and Papers, Foreign and Domestic, Henry VIII,* Volume 5, n. 216.
[4] Ibid., n. 238.
[5] Anna Whitelock, *Mary Tudor: England's First Queen,* pp. 46, 51.
[6] *Letters and Papers, Henry VIII,* Volume 5, n. 1377.
[7] *Calendar of State Papers, Spain,* Volume 4 Part 2, n. 1100.
[8] *Calendar of State Papers, Spain,* Volume 5 Part 1, n. 22.
[9] Ibid.
[10] *Letters and Papers, Henry VIII,* Volume 7, n. 232.
[11] *Letters and Papers, Foreign and Domestic, Henry VIII,* Volume 13 Part 2, n. 800.
[12] Ibid.
[13] Ibid., Volume 7, n. 980.
[14] Ibid., n. 1193.

Chapter 3:
"As long as that woman lived"

Anne Boleyn's failure to give Henry VIII a longed-for son only increased her fierce pride for her only child, Princess Elizabeth. Until Anne became pregnant again, Elizabeth was the focus of her maternal feelings. Anne dreamed of a French marriage for Elizabeth and picked one of Francis I's sons, the Duke of Angoulême, who seemed a suitable match for the little princess. Anne encouraged the French ambassadors to visit her daughter, but the French had no inclination to do so of their own volition because they believed Elizabeth was illegitimate and thus not a match for their King's son. In October 1535, they told the imperial ambassador Chapuys that they went to see Elizabeth only because of "the frequent importunities of her mother".[1] Anne was well aware that Francis I would rather match his son with Lady Mary, and she was eager to show Mary her place and tightened the grip of security around her. Chapuys picked up a rumour that Anne was becoming increasingly worried that she was still not pregnant and had bribed a soothsayer to prophesy that she would not conceive another child as long as Katharine of Aragon and her daughter were alive.

Although the 1534 Act of Succession was enforced by an oath of allegiance promulgated by Parliament in the same year, neither Katharine nor Mary yielded. Refusal was equivalent to treason; the most famous victims of the act were Bishop John Fisher and Sir Thomas More, who refused to accept Henry VIII as head of the Anglican Church and swear an oath to uphold the Act of Succession passed in March. They refused to take the oath because it included the abjuration of the pope's authority. Fisher and More were executed on 22 June and 6 July 1535 respectively.

Lady Mary was pressured to accept the new political and religious situation, but she steadfastly refused to acknowledge Anne as Queen. Anne Shelton, the Queen's aunt, informed Mary that "the King himself has said that he would make her lose her head for violating the laws of his realm", but Mary remained undaunted, or at least she appeared so to the outside world.[2] In reality, she suffered from irregular, painful menstruations and severe depression. "Her treatment would suffice to make a healthy person ill", Katharine of Aragon complained to Charles V.[3] Katharine now believed that she and her daughter would "be sentenced to martyrdom, which she was ready to receive in testimony of the Holy Faith, as the cardinal of Rochester and other holy martyrs had done". It was Katharine's wish to die "in sight of the people" and enter the pages of history as a martyr who fought for her marriage and faith.

Her mother's stance made a deep impact on Mary, who firmly believed her life was also in danger. Someone close to the royal circles informed Mary that Anne Boleyn often boasted that she would poison her. "She is my death and I am hers", was Anne's favourite saying.[4] These threats pushed Mary to fear for her life and hate Anne Boleyn even more intensely. On one occasion, Mary informed the imperial ambassador Chapuys that she had "full confidence in God that she will go straight to Paradise and be quit of the tribulations of this world, and her only grief is about the troubles of the Queen her mother".[5] She sought solace in her Catholic faith, becoming increasingly pious and conservative in her views. But her health was deteriorating, as always when she was under strain. She became evermore suspicious and careful in choosing friends she confided in and started suffering from insomnia that would accompany her in times of stress for the rest of her life.

Despite Mary's fear for Katharine of Aragon's life, the former Queen's well-being was never in any danger, and she lacked no luxuries in her exile. Although Katharine complained to Charles V that she was ready to "go sue for alms for the love of God", she sat at the centre of a household costing Henry VIII a little under £3,000.[6] Besides ladies-in-waiting, a lord chamberlain, a physician, an almoner and an apothecary, Katharine had servants who worked in various divisions of her household, such as the bakehouse, buttery, kitchen, acatry (a separate department responsible for supplying meat and fish), poultry, scullery and saucery (this department provided thick condiments eaten cold with the meat and fish). She had her own stables and wardrobe from where she ordered clothes for herself and livery for her servants. In December of 1534, Katharine's chamberlain received £500 for the auxiliary expenses of her household. In the period just from 19 December 1534 to 30 September 1535, the expenses of Katharine's household "above stairs" consumed £2,926.[7] We could compare that to the expenses of Katharine's household when she was Queen between the years 1525 and 1529. From March 1524 to March 1525, for instance, the sum paid for her household totalled £4,440. In subsequent years, the sum was similar, rarely exceeding the

£4,000 mark.[8] The cost of Katharine's household as Dowager Princess of Wales was cut in half since the King reduced the number of servants she had, but, nevertheless, her new establishment was still royal. In the summer of 1536, Cromwell rightly observed that Henry "has maintained the great and sumptuous house of the lady Katharine Dowager".[9] In August 1535, Henry VIII paid Edmund Bedingfield, Katharine's chamberlain, £533 "for the Princess Dowager's Household".[10] Katharine was not a queen anymore, but as the Dowager Princess of Wales she was still treated as a member of the royal family.

Mary, too, did not lack for luxuries. Her household was divided into similar divisions as her mother's. In the period from 1 October 1533 to 30 September 1534, Mary's entire household totalled £2,901.[11] Her establishment was headed by a chamberlain and vice-chamberlain. She had two chaplains, two yeomen, two grooms and two gentleman ushers. At her table, she was served by a cupbearer, two sewers, a sewer of the chamber and five gentleman waiters. In addition, her "above stairs" household was staffed with yeomen of the chamber, groom porters, grooms of the chamber and a clerk comptroller. There were also two gentlewomen and two chamberers, performing menial tasks such as changing linen, cleaning and refreshing Mary's apartments and emptying chamber pots, and a laundress. Mary also had ladies-in-waiting and maids, girls and young women of noble birth who accompanied her in daily activities. Among them were Margaret Douglas, Mary's first cousin and personal friend, Frances Elmer, Anne Hussey and Mary Browne. Mary continued her education under the auspices of Richard Featherstone and was free to read books she liked and order whatever clothes she wanted. She also had her own minstrels who played while she ate or during her daily activities, such as reading and sewing, and during feasts such as Christmas. In total, there were 162 persons in Mary's establishment.[12]

Mary's and Katharine's problem was that they didn't want to accept their demoted positions. They were both stripped of the vestiges of royalty, such as the crown jewels they were both entitled to wear as Queen and heiress to the throne, but not as the Dowager Princess of Wales and the King's illegitimate daughter, and made great show of refusing to part with them. Katharine's crown jewels were taken away from her in the summer of 1532 when the King bestowed them on Anne Boleyn before their trip to Calais. Katharine was reluctant and replied that "it was against her conscience to give her jewels to adorn a person who is the scandal of Christendom, and a disgrace to the King", but she eventually gave them up after seeing her husband's handwritten command.[13] Yet Katharine withheld some pieces that were confiscated by Henry VIII in April of 1533 and delivered to Sir Richard Page, gentleman of the King's Privy Chamber, by Katharine's lady-in-waiting Blanche Twyford.[14] Similarly, when in August 1533 the King ordered Mary's governess, Lady Salisbury, to make an inventory of Mary's crown jewels and deliver them into the custody of Frances Elmer, the governess refused, doubtless on Mary's request.[15] In February 1534, when Mary found herself "destitute of clothes and other necessaries", she send a messenger to her father, requesting the King send her either money or new clothes. The messenger was instructed to accept the King's gifts only if the issued warrant named Mary as princess—a task that was doomed to fail from the start.[16]

By December 1535, Katharine of Aragon's health was rapidly deteriorating. Eustace Chapuys, who visited the former Queen as she lay dying at Kimbolton Castle, reported that she suffered from "a pain in the stomach, so violent that she could retain no food". The imperial ambassador quizzed Katharine's Spanish physician as to whether he suspected poisoning. Miguel de la Soa believed that it was likely that Katharine may have been administered "a slow and subtle poison for he could not discover evidences of simple and pure poison".[17] Shortly before her death, Katharine of Aragon's last thoughts turned to her daughter. In a letter to Henry VIII, the former Queen besought him to be a good father to Mary:

"My most dear lord, King and husband,

The hour of my death now drawing on, the tender love I owe you forceth me, my case being such, to commend myself to you, and to put you in remembrance with a few words of the health and safeguard of your soul which you ought to prefer before all worldly matters, and before the care and pampering of your body, for the which you have cast me into many calamities and yourself into many troubles. For my part, I pardon you everything, and I wish to devoutly pray God that He will pardon you also.

For the rest, I commend unto you our daughter Mary, beseeching you to be a good father unto her, as I have heretofore desired. I entreat you also, on behalf of my maids, to give them marriage portions, which is not much, they being but three. For all my other servants, I solicit the wages due them, and a year more, lest they be unprovided for. Lastly, I make this vow, that mine eyes desire you above all things.

Katharine the Quene."[18]

It has been recently suggested that the letter is a product of later Catholic propaganda and is, therefore, "almost certainly fictitious".[19] However, the letter written by Katharine shortly before her death is mentioned in a contemporary source describing her funeral procession. The anonymous author was disgusted that rumours alleging "that in the hour of death, she acknowledged she had not been Queen of England" were spread in England shortly after Katharine's demise. He knew that it was not true "because at that hour, she ordered a writing to be made in her name addressed to the King as her husband, and to the ambassador of the Emperor, her nephew, which she signed with these words: Katharine, Queen of England, commending her ladies and servants to the favour of the said ambassador".[20]

Since Katharine maintained that she was Henry VIII's wife, she was not entitled to compose her last will, as married women could not make such a document. Instead, she drafted a document resembling a testament, wherein she made her wishes concerning her daughter, servants, debts and possessions. In the document, she bequeathed to her daughter a collar she had brought from Spain, a golden cross with a piece of the Lignum Crucis—wood from the True Cross—and what was left of her once vast collection of expensive furs.[21] The cross, Katharine's last gift to Mary, was detained by the King's secretary, Thomas Cromwell, on Henry VIII's request.[22] Katharine of Aragon died on 7 January 1536, calling herself Henry VIII's wife until the end. As soon as the former Queen died, Eustace Chapuys wrote a letter to Mary informing her about the event in the most delicate and empathetic way, hoping to be the first person to inform Mary of her mother's death. The letter was given to one of Mary's trusted maids, who passed it on to her at the ambassador's command. Mary drew consolation from Chapuys's letter and began writing to him more often than she used to, perceiving him as a friend and a link to her late mother.

Whereas Mary thought about her mother as "having always been her principal refuge in all her tribulations", Henry VIII was more than happy to be rid of the mother of his eldest child.[23] Only a day after Katharine's death he organised a lavish banquet and joust at Greenwich and ceremoniously paraded with Princess Elizabeth in his arms. Chapuys was disgusted when he reported that the King was "clad all over in yellow, from top to toe, except the white feather he had in his bonnet".[24] It is sometimes erroneously suggested that yellow was a colour of mourning in Spain and Henry demonstrated respect for Katharine's death by dressing in this colour.[25] Yellow was associated, in England and in Spain, with hope and joy. The author of the anonymous *Spanish Chronicle* was certain that the King's choice of garment for this occasion was a calculated insult to the memory of his late wife since "yellow in that country [England] is a sign of rejoicing".[26] Whether Anne also wore a yellow dress remains unclear. Her most vociferous critic, Chapuys, didn't even mention Anne's presence during the banquet and celebratory joust, and when the King fell from his horse on the tiltyard, it was the Duke of Norfolk who brought her the news, suggesting that Anne wasn't there. Chronicler Edward Hall, however, wrote that "Queen Anne wore yellow for the mourning", and Nicholas Sander, hostile as he was, repeated after the chronicler, writing that "instead of putting on mourning on the day of Katharine's funeral, [Anne] put on a yellow dress".[27]

Anne, who was expecting her third child at the time, decided that her rival's death was an occasion to mend fences with Mary and reached out to her. Anne promised that if Mary laid her obstinacy aside, she would become "her warmest friend, and a second mother". If only Mary would become a "dutiful daughter", she might return to court as member of the royal family and be exempted from being Anne's trainbearer, walking beside her like her equal.[28] Mary refused to countenance the offer of a woman who celebrated her mother's death by wearing a yellow dress and handsomely rewarding the messenger who brought her the news of Katharine's passing.

Since Katharine of Aragon was dead, Mary could not state that she recognised no other Queen than her mother, but she now decided, with Chapuys's help, that since the pope had determined in 1534 that Henry VIII's marriage to Katharine of Aragon was lawful and his marriage to Anne Boleyn was not, "the Lady Anne could never assume the title of Queen". Furthermore, Chapuys advised Mary to say that "she could not conscientiously contravene the Pope's commands".[29] According to the laws established by Henry VIII, his daughter was now committing an act of treason, favouring a foreign power (the pope) over her father's authority. Anne Boleyn was well aware that if she had a son, the King would imprison Mary or threaten her with execution, and the blame would, as always, fall on her. She decided to beg Mary to reconsider her overtures of friendship. In a letter addressed to Anne Shelton deliberately left in Mary's oratory, Anne informed her aunt that the King planned to bring the matter of his elder daughter's disobedience to an end:

"What I have done has been more for charity than for anything the King or I care what road she [Mary] takes, or whether she will change her purpose, for if I have a son, as I hope shortly, I know what will happen to her; and therefore, considering the Word of God, to do good to one's enemy, I wished to warn her beforehand because I have daily experience that the King's wisdom is such as not to esteem her repentance of her rudeness and unnatural obstinacy when she has no choice."[30]

Anne implied that she was giving Mary a chance to accept the political reality because if she had a son, the King would act more decisively and would not tolerate Mary's obstinacy any longer. Sadly, Anne's hopes of having a baby boy never came to fruition. On 29 January 1536, just as Katharine of Aragon's lifeless body was laid to rest beneath the cold pavement of Peterborough Cathedral, Anne miscarried a son. Usually, news about such intimate details from behind closed doors were kept secret, but this time the Queen's miscarriage became the subject of vitriolic gossip. Many, including the King himself, believed that Anne was unable to bear male children. Some even implied she had only pretended to have been with child.

Anne Boleyn's days as Henry VIII's wife were numbered. The King was no longer in love with the once-cherished Anne and started courting one of her maids of honour, Jane Seymour. Jane was coached by Anne's enemies to refuse to yield to the King's passion. Using the same tactic Anne had ten years earlier, Jane desperately clung to her virtue and refused to sleep with the King. By April 1536, Mary was informed by her friends who conspired against Anne Boleyn that "very shortly her rival would be dismissed".[31] Mary took a keen interest in the unfolding conspiracy and firmly believed that her father would soon divorce Anne. She instructed Eustace Chapuys to "watch the proceedings, and if possible help to accomplish the said divorce".[32]

It is evident that neither Mary nor Anne Boleyn's enemies were aware of what was about to happen. They often used the words "dismiss" and "divorce" interchangeably when speaking about Anne's ruin. This clearly points out that they expected Henry VIII to divorce Anne and send her away from court in disgrace. At some point, however, the conspiracy turned deadly. Anne was arrested on 2 May 1536 on multiple charges of adultery, incest and plotting the King's death. She was executed on 19 May, the first English Queen consort to be put to death.

Anne saw Elizabeth for the last time in late April of 1536. Alexander Alesius, a Scottish theologian who resided at court at the time, witnessed a dramatic scene as he passed through the courtyard at Greenwich Palace. Years later, he wrote to Elizabeth of what he had seen:

"Never shall I forget the sorrow which I felt when I saw the most serene Queen, your most religious mother, carrying you, still a little baby, in her arms and entreating the most serene King, your father, in Greenwich Palace, from the open window of which he was looking into the courtyard, when she brought you to him. I did not perfectly understand what had been going on, but the faces and gestures of the speakers plainly showed that the King was angry, although he could conceal his anger wonderfully well."[33]

Anne's desperate attempt to secure an audience with her royal husband proves just how isolated she must have felt. Perhaps she took Elizabeth into her arms to appeal to the King's fatherly feelings. There were rumours swirling that Anne had been unfaithful and Elizabeth was not Henry VIII's daughter, but a changeling or a child of the

King's Groom of the Stool, Henry Norris. Anne was desperate to give lie to such slanders, showing off Elizabeth with her curly red hair inherited from the King.

Anne was well aware that something sinister was happening around her, and, six days before her arrest, she summoned her favourite chaplain for a private audience. Matthew Parker was Anne's "poor countryman", hailing from the Queen's native county of Kent. Anne entrusted her daughter's spiritual well-being to him, a heartfelt plea that made its indelible mark on Parker's memory. Many years later, when he became Elizabeth's first Archbishop of Canterbury, he declared that "if I had not been so much bound to the mother, I would not so soon have granted to serve her daughter in this place".[34] He kept Anne Boleyn's portrait in his episcopal palace of Lambeth, a reminder of his promise.

Mary now hoped that Anne's death would pave the way towards her reconciliation with the King. "I perceived that nobody dared speak for me as long as that woman lived, which now is gone; whom I pray our Lord of his great mercy to forgive", she wrote to Thomas Cromwell.[35] A story originated in the eighteenth century that Anne had thrown herself on her knees before Lady Kingston, who attended her in the Tower, and requested her "to go in her name to the Lady Mary, to kneel before her in like manner, and beg of her to pardon an unfortunate woman the many wrongs she had done her".[36] Whether Anne truly asked for Mary's forgiveness may never be known, but what we do know is that Mary loathed Anne to the end of her life.

Henry VIII married his mistress, Jane Seymour, on 30 May 1536. Mary, still living in a joint household with Elizabeth, naively believed that her father would soon send for her and she would resume the life of a royal princess and heiress to the throne. Mary's friends and allies, including the King's Master of the Horse, Sir Nicholas Carew, believed that she was "a meet person to be an heir apparent" if Jane Seymour failed to give birth to a son.[37] Mary herself certainly thought so, but she was soon to be disillusioned. It was a rude awakening for Mary when she realised that it was her father, not Anne Boleyn, who had obstructed the reconciliation.

Jane Seymour made all the efforts she could muster to convince the King to reinstate Mary to the succession and invite her to court, but he wanted Mary to accept that she was his illegitimate daughter first. The King was a vain man who hated the idea of a political party clustering around his widely popular twenty-year-old daughter, whom many perceived as his rightful heiress. He was bent on forcing Mary to accept that his marriage to her mother was invalid. Mary could hardly believe this. She knew that Jane Seymour had initiated the process of reconciliation, and in a letter to the new Queen, she described herself as her "most humble and obedient daughter and handmaid".[38]

What Mary did not know was that Henry VIII had "rudely repulsed" his new Queen when he perceived she was too vocal in her support of Mary.[39] Jane's efforts on Mary's behalf always irritated the King, who once called his wife a fool for trying to speak up for his elder daughter. She should, he warned her, think about their future offspring and not any other children. Sir Nicholas Carew also tasted the King's wrath and wrote hurriedly to Mary, advising her to conform to her father's wishes, for "if [she will] not submit herself she is undone".[40] Mary, threatened by the arrests of her supporters and frightened by the possibility of losing her head, signed the document acknowledging that her parents' marriage was invalid, thus rendering herself the King's illegitimate daughter. She also accepted the King as the Supreme Head of the Church in England and repudiated "the pretended authority of the bishop of Rome".[41] Everything she and Katharine of Aragon had fought for with such vehemence over the past three years

"As long as that woman lived"

vanished with one stroke of the pen. By 6 July 1536, Mary was reconciled with the King her father, and was presented to Queen Jane as her stepdaughter.

A contemporary *Cronica del Rey Enrico Ottavo da Inglaterra* (*Chronicle of King Henry VIII of England*), written by an anonymous Spaniard in the 1550s and thus commonly known as *The Spanish Chronicle*, gives details of their encounter. The chronicle, often attributed to Antonio de Guaras, a Spanish merchant who lived in London in the 1530s, is not the most reliable of sources, but it offers a reflection of contemporary thought. Peppered with snippets of conversations that were undoubtedly based on contemporary rumours and knowledge gleaned from the people who came into contact with the chronicler, *The Spanish Chronicle* should be viewed with a dose of scepticism at times since it is biased in favour of the Spanish Katharine of Aragon and those who held pro-imperial views, but it should never be dismissed as completely unreliable.

According to the chronicle, when Henry VIII met Mary in July of 1536, he said: "My daughter, she [Anne Boleyn] who did you so much harm, and prevented me from seeing you for so long, has paid the penalty."[42] Then Jane

Seymour knelt down and addressed the King: "Your Majesty knows how bad Queen Anne was, and it is not fit that her daughter should be the Princess." Hearing this, the King "ordered it to be proclaimed that in future none should dare to call her Princess, but Madam Elizabeth".[43] This, of course, was wishful thinking on the chronicler's part. Henry VIII could never publicly admit that he was led by Anne Boleyn, and his harsh treatment of Mary preceding their meeting proves that he had been in charge all along. Also, he decided to brand Elizabeth as illegitimate without Jane Seymour's interference since Henry's annulment of his marriage to Anne automatically meant that their child was illegitimate.

However, other sources indicate that Mary blamed Anne Boleyn for the rest of her life, and it is not inconceivable that she and Jane Seymour both believed that Anne was a "bad" person and the wicked driving force behind many of the King's decisions during the period from 1526 to 1536, most notably the split from Rome. The sentence inserted into Henry's mouth—"she who did you so much harm, and prevented me from seeing you for so long, has paid the penalty"—mirrors Mary's own statement expressed in a letter to Cromwell that "nobody dared speak for me as long as that woman lived".[44] It is thus highly likely that the sentiments expressed in *The Spanish Chronicle* were real, with the exception that they were expressed in private and not in public.

NOTES

[1] *Calendar of State Papers, Spain,* Volume 5 Part 1, n. 213.
[2] *Letters and Papers, Henry VIII,* Volume 7, n. 530.
[3] Ibid., Volume 8, n. 514.
[4] Ibid., Volume 9, n. 873.
[5] Ibid., Volume 7, n. 662.
[6] *Letters and Papers, Foreign and Domestic, Henry VIII,* Volume 8, n. 514.
[7] Ibid., Volume 7, n. 1208.
[8] Ibid., Volume 8, n. 6121.
[9] Ibid., Volume 10, n. 1231.
[10] Ibid., Volume 9, n. 217.
[11] Ibid., Volume 6, n. 1185.
[12] Ibid., n. 1199.
[13] Ibid., Volume 5, n. 1377.
[14] TNA E 101/421/7.
[15] *Letters and Papers, Foreign and Domestic, Henry VIII,* Volume 6, n. 1009.
[16] Ibid., Volume 8, n. 214.
[17] Ibid., Volume 10, n. 59.
[18] Patrick Williams, *Katharine of Aragon*, p. 374.
[19] Giles Tremlett, *Catherine of Aragon*, p. 422.
[20] *Letters and Papers, Henry VIII,* Volume 10, n. 284.
[21] *Calendar of State Papers, Spain,* Volume 5 Part 2, n. 37.
[22] Ibid., n. 29.
[23] Ibid., n. 9.
[24] *Letters and Papers, Henry VIII,* Volume 10, n. 141.
[25] In *Six Wives of Henry VIII*, Alison Weir stated that Henry and Anne donned yellow as a mark of respect for Katharine because yellow was "the colour of royal mourning in Spain" (p. 299). However, she corrected this in *The Lady In The Tower: The Fall of Anne Boleyn*, stating that it is "a misconception that yellow was the colour of Spanish Royal mourning" (p. 21).
[26] *Chronicle of King Henry VIII*, p. 52
[27] Nicholas Sander, *The Rise and Growth of the Anglican Schism*, p. 132. Edward Hall, *Hall's Chronicle*, p. 818.
[28] *Calendar of State Papers, Spain,* Volume 5 Part 2, n. 9.

[29] Ibid.
[30] *Letters and Papers, Henry VIII*, Volume 10, n. 307.
[31] *Calendar of State Papers, Spain*, Volume 5 Part 2, n. 47.
[32] Ibid., n. 48.
[33] *Calendar of State Papers Foreign, Elizabeth*, Volume 1: 1558–1559, n. 1303.
[34] John Bruce (ed.)., *Correspondence of Matthew Parker*, p. 391.
[35] *Letters and Papers, Henry VIII*, Volume 10, n. 968.
[36] John Lingard, *The History of England*, Volume 4, p. 244.
[37] *Letters and Papers, Henry VIII*, Volume 10, n. 1134.
[38] M. A. Everett Wood, *Letters of Royal and Illustrious Ladies of Great Britain*, Volume 2, p. 263.
[39] *Letters and Papers, Henry VIII*, Volume 11, n. 7.
[40] *Letters and Papers, Henry VIII*, Volume 10, n. 1134.
[41] Ibid., n. 1137.
[42] M.A.Sharp Hume (ed.), *Chronicle of King Henry VIII (The Spanish Chronicle)*, p. 72.
[43] Ibid., p. 73.
[44] Quoted earlier in this chapter.

Chapter 4: "Concerning the Princess"

In the summer of 1536, just as the new Act of Succession declaring both of Henry VIII's daughters illegitimate was being prepared, Mary was still residing with Elizabeth in their joint household, moving between royal residences at Hunsdon and Hatfield. In a letter she penned to Thomas Cromwell in June 1536, shortly after she grasped that she must submit to the King's will, she broached the subject of Elizabeth and her legitimacy:

"Frist, concerning the Princess (so I think I must call her yet, for I would be loath to offend), I offered at her entry to that name and honour [in 1533], to call her sister, but it was refused unless I would also add the other title unto it, which I denied, not then more obstinately than I am now sorry for it, for that I did therein offend my most gracious father and his just laws. And now that you think it meet [wise], I shall never call her by other name than sister."[1]

To please her father, Mary decided to show him that she treated Elizabeth as her half sister and harboured no ill feelings towards her. On 21 July 1536, Mary informed the King that "my sister Elizabeth is in good health (thanks to our Lord) and such a child toward, as I doubt not, but your Highness shall have cause to rejoice of in time coming (as knoweth Almighty God), who send your Grace, with the Queen my good mother, health, with the accomplishments of your desires".[2]

Anne Boleyn's death on the scaffold did not change Henry VIII's attitude towards their daughter, although at the time of Anne's downfall rumours circulated at court that Elizabeth was not the King's child, but a "daughter of Master Norris", who was executed as one of five putative lovers of Queen Anne.[3] Henry VIII clearly did not believe this, but Mary entertained doubts as to whether Elizabeth was truly her half sister. Later in her life Mary would tell her ladies that Elizabeth "had the face and countenance of Mark Smeaton", a handsome musician who was executed as one of Anne Boleyn's lovers.[4] At the time, however, Mary knew that the King loved Elizabeth, and so she praised her to him in the abovementioned letter, keeping her true feelings to herself.

In October 1536, the two girls were invited to court and treated honourably by their father. The French ambassador reported that Mary was now "first after the

Queen, and sits at table opposite her, a little lower down, after having first given the napkin for washing to the King and Queen". The three-year-old Elizabeth did not sit at the table with the adults, but the ambassador recorded that "the King is very affectionate to her. It is said he loves her much".[5] Mary, at twenty, was a frequent visitor to Henry VIII's exuberant court, and she built a network of strong alliances and friendships, some of which were to last until the end of her life. Among her close friends was Queen Jane, her new stepmother. In December 1536, Mary accompanied the royal couple as they rode in a triumphant procession over the frozen Thames and celebrated Christmas with them at Greenwich Palace. It was Mary's first taste of family life since 1531, when her life as a cherished royal princess was abruptly shattered by the discord between her parents.

Mary's submission to Henry VIII's will was rewarded with the appointment of a new household and arrangement for a regular pension to cover her servants' wages and personal needs. The new provision was for twenty-nine servants, four ladies-in-waiting, two chamberers, five gentlemen, five yeomen, four grooms, four grooms of the stable, a physician, a chaplain, a footman, a woodbearer and a laundress.[6] In the aftermath of Elizabeth's birth, Mary had lost her trusted female attendants and was now glad to welcome them back into her service. The King consulted Mary and asked which women she would like to appoint. In a letter to Cromwell, Mary replied:

"Touching the nomination of such women as I would have about me, I am content with what men or women the King will appoint me; but I think Margery Baynton and Susan Clarencius ought to be considered for their faithful service to the King and me since they came unto my company. I should also be glad to have Mary Brown, sometime my maid."[7]

Mary's request was granted, and Susan Clarencius and Margery Baynton entered her new household, but Mary Brown did not. Brown could have been the confidential maid who was dismissed from Mary's service in 1534. That maid, whose identity remains unknown, staunchly refused to swear the oath accepting Princess Elizabeth as heiress to the crown and was threatened with imprisonment. She eventually swore the oath but kept working for Mary, smuggling letters from the imperial ambassador and other people. She was dismissed in the spring of 1534, much to Mary's disappointment. If Mary Brown was the dismissed maid, Mary's request to reappoint her seems all the more poignant since Brown had displeased the King. Frances

Elmer and Frances Baynham were also appointed as Mary's ladies, as were Anne Morgan, Mary Finch, Frances Jerningham and Elizabeth Sidney.[8]

Although still proclaimed illegitimate, Mary's prospects changed for the better in 1536. Her Privy Purse expenses reveal that she was often at court, having her own lodgings there in February 1537 and spending Easter at Greenwich with the King and Queen. She stood as godmother to numerous children, a sign that many courtiers perceived her as influential, and had enough money to purchase new clothes and jewels. In October 1537, Mary stood as godmother to the most important infant in England—Prince Edward, the son of Henry VIII and Jane Seymour. Mary's Privy Purse expenses show that she gave handsome rewards to the midwife, wet nurse and rockers of the cradle and ordered an elaborate kirtle of cloth of silver for the christening.

The christening was a lavish ceremony held in the royal chapel at Hampton Court. A large octagonal platform was raised in the centre of the chapel so that everyone could see the King of England's heir being anointed by the Archbishop of Canterbury. Prince Edward was carried by Gertrude Courtenay, Marchioness of Exeter, who was supported by her husband and the Duke of Suffolk on each side. Several nobles carried a canopy of estate over him. The long train of the prince's baptismal gown was carried by the Earl of Arundel and Lord William Howard. Many nobles walked in procession to the chapel: the Earl of Sussex and Baron Montague bearing "a pair of covered basins", the Earl of Wiltshire (Anne Boleyn's father), carrying a "taper of virgin wax" and a "towel about his neck", the Earl of Essex holding "a salt of gold", and Edward Seymour, Viscount Beauchamp, holding Lady Elizabeth in his arms. Elizabeth was too small to walk by herself and carry a heavy ceremonial "crysome richly garnished". Mary walked directly after Prince Edward, and the long train of her gown was carried by her old friend Lady Mary Kingston.

After the ceremony was over, the prince was carried to his parents, who had not attended the christening but awaited him in the antechamber. A small banquet followed afterwards with spices, wafers and wine served to the most important nobles. Mary and Elizabeth each had their own cupbearers. Lord Dacre of the South carried spice plates to both, Baron Cobham performed the same function with wafers and Baron Montague ceremonially uncovered the spice plates. It was an elaborate ritual that emphasised the fact that Mary and Elizabeth, although illegitimate, were still the King's daughters. With the banquet over, the procession wound its way back to the palace "saving that the taper, salt and basin were left and the gifts of the gossips [godparents] carried".[9] Mary's gift to the prince, a cup of gold, was carried by Henry Bourchier, Earl of Essex. Mary went holding Elizabeth's hand, the train of her gown carried by Lady Herbert of Troy, mistress of Elizabeth's new household.

The birth of a son finally gave Henry VIII the male heir for whom he had ruined so many lives, including those of his daughters and their mothers. With a healthy son and a prospect of more children by Jane Seymour, it seemed that Mary's chance of ever becoming Queen was slim. She and Elizabeth were now not only illegitimate but also highly unlikely to inherit the throne. Ironically, this fact seemed to draw the Tudor half sisters closer together, removing the aspect of rivalry from their relationship. Two weeks after Prince Edward's birth, however, their lives were turned upside down yet again when Jane Seymour died as a result of postnatal complications. For the previous eighteen months, it was Jane who had given both Mary and Elizabeth a sense of familial stability, and she would have likely continued to do so had she lived longer.

Jane Seymour's generosity towards Mary often overshadows her relationship with Anne Boleyn's daughter, but it is clear that although she had a closer relationship with Mary due to their respective ages and religious views, she was not indifferent towards Elizabeth. A *Book of the Queen's Jewels*—an inventory of valuables owned by Queen Jane and given as gifts to her favourites—reveals that she often presented both Mary and Elizabeth with valuable trinkets such as beads, pomanders and girdles. Further accounts of the Queen's wardrobe reveal that she provided Elizabeth with items of clothing, such as Scottish bonnets and linen. She also paid for Elizabeth's New Year's gift in 1537 and gave money to Elizabeth Cavendish, who served in Elizabeth's household.

Mary was appointed to serve as chief mourner during the Queen's funeral, riding on horseback behind the hearse carrying Jane's lifeless body, but she was so distraught that she only attended one day, and her place was later taken by Frances Grey, Marchioness of Dorset. Mary was heartbroken and gave presents of money to the Queen's three chamberers, her page, footman and gardener.[10] She also gave offerings during the Masses for the Queen's soul. Mary was so depressed after Jane's funeral that the late Queen's sister-in-law, Anne,

Viscountess Beauchamp, sent her daughter accompanied by a nurse to lift Mary's spirits.

The anonymous author of *The Spanish Chronicle* correctly observed that Queen Jane "was also deeply mourned by Madam Mary; and the King ordered that the ladies-in-waiting should remain with her, and, until he married again, they remained in attendance on her, and treated her as if she were Queen".[11] From October 1537 to January 1540, there was no Queen to serve, but Mary effectively took the part of a royal consort and was served by a host of ladies-in-waiting who had previously staffed the Queen's Privy Chamber. Mary made close friendships with some of them, including Anne Seymour, who would become her "good Nan" in spite of the religious differences between them. Despite her illegitimacy, foreign ambassadors (especially those sent by Charles V) still referred to Mary as "princess". In her early twenties, Mary was an attractive marriage prospect, and the King dangled her hand as a prize on the international marriage market to build new alliances. On 2 March 1538, Eustace Chapuys described his visit to the royal children. Prince Edward and "Madame Isabelle", as he referred to Elizabeth, were living together at Eltham Palace, whereas Mary was residing at

Richmond. Chapuys praised Mary's ability to play the lute and spinet.[12]

Mary, who hoped to be married off soon, was preparing to visit court for the Easter celebrations and was eager to know what colour of clothes she should wear; whether she should still appear in black, mourning Queen Jane, or something more cheerful like her gown of white taffeta edged with velvet that the King liked so much and that "suited to this joyful feast of our Lord's holy rising from the dead". The King replied rather indifferently that she should wear whatever she liked.[13] On 5 May 1538, the King paid a cordial visit to Mary at Richmond, where they dined together.[14]

Less than ten days later, the King found his life in peril. The years of misuse of his body and the dangerous fall he suffered when jousting on 24 January 1536 were beginning to show on his ever-expanding frame. The King's legs had a tendency to swell, and they were covered in fistulas. In May 1538, one of the fistulas closed up, and the King remained speechless for almost two weeks, "black in the face and in great danger". The royal physicians lanced the fistula with a red-hot poker, allowing drainage of the "humours" and saving the King's life. From that point on, the fistulas were kept open for the King's safety, producing a putrid stench that could be identified three rooms away, often announcing Henry's arrival.[15]

Despite his health problems, Henry VIII remarried in 1540, taking Anne of Cleves from Germany as his fourth bride. The marriage was annulled after six months, and the King married Katherine Howard, a teenaged cousin of Anne Boleyn. This marriage ended in Katherine's execution on 13 February 1542, after it had been discovered that she was not a virgin when she married Henry VIII and may have had an extramarital affair with one of the King's favourites, Thomas Culpeper. Although it seemed as if the grief-stricken Henry VIII would never remarry after Katherine's execution, in 1543 he decided to marry Katherine Parr, a comely widow in her early thirties.

Elizabeth, then ten years old, and Mary, twenty-seven, were among twelve guests who gathered in the royal chapel at Hampton Court on 12 July 1543 to witness their father's wedding. Both Mary and Elizabeth formed a close relationship with their new stepmother, but it was the impressionable Elizabeth who quickly became fascinated with the Queen. During the summer and early autumn of 1544, she joined Katherine Parr's household as her "ordinary" maid of honour, which means that she served the Queen on a daily basis. Henry VIII was on a war campaign in France at the time, and Elizabeth had a rare chance to observe Katherine Parr exercising her political role as regent.[16]

In 1544, Henry VIII decided to include Mary and Elizabeth in the new Act of Succession. This is often attributed to the influence of the King's sixth wife, Katherine Parr, who treated both of his daughters with kindness, although the King had planned to include them in the succession to bolster their eligibility on the international marriage market before he married Katherine. They were still deemed as his illegitimate daughters—they had never recovered the title of princess—but their royal status was confirmed.

To celebrate the new act and memorialise his daughters' restoration to the line of succession, Henry VIII commissioned the famous Whitehall family portrait. The portrait captures the royal family in a private setting, with the King sitting in the centre beneath a canopy of state, flanked by his son and heir, Edward, on the left and his third wife, the late Jane Seymour, on the right. The King's hand rests firmly on Edward's shoulder, showing quite literally that Henry VIII's dynastic hopes now rested on the shoulders of a single surviving son. The King is richly bedecked in a splendid costume of cloth of gold and red with a knee-length cloak furred with sables. Jane Seymour wears a matching gown of cloth of gold, with red sleeves and kirtle. Her large oversleeves and the edge of her gown are furred with ermine, a symbol of wealth and royalty. The inclusion of Jane Seymour rather than Katherine Parr showed that Henry VIII desired Jane to be regarded as the matriarch of the Tudor dynasty.

Elizabeth stands on the far right while Mary occupies the far place on the left. Their costumes are far more modest than those worn by Henry VIII and Jane Seymour, but they match Prince Edward's outfit in terms of colour and fabric. They are wearing dark-patterned gowns with red undersleeves and kirtles. There is nothing remarkable about their costumes—the gowns look rather simple and are calculated to blend in with the dark background. What draws the viewer's attention are the jewels. Upon closer inspection, it appears that Elizabeth wears a golden letter *A* suspended from a double strand of pearls with large pearl hanging down from an emerald within the letter. In *Tudor Costume and Fashion*, Herbert Norris suggested that the necklace belonged to Elizabeth's mother, the executed Anne Boleyn.[17] This suggestion may be close to the truth. Mary wears a similar pearl necklace;

suspended from it is a golden cross with three hanging pearls. It is known that Mary received "a necklace with a cross" from her dying mother; was it the same necklace worn by Mary in this family portrait?[18] Let's think about it; both Mary and Elizabeth were memorialised in this painting as Henry VIII's illegitimate daughters. They stood to inherit the crown if their half brother, Edward, died without issue. Such a turn of events seemed unlikely at the time, hence the positioning of the Tudor half sisters at the far ends of the painting. Both Mary and Elizabeth wear similar gowns—at first glance they look almost like twins. This type of representation may have served to emphasise their status as the King's illegitimate daughters. In this context, it made sense to allow Mary and Elizabeth to wear jewellery belonging to their disfavoured mothers, whose marriages to Henry VIII were annulled in 1533 and 1536 respectively.

At the time when Mary and Elizabeth were reinstated to the line of succession, their father was already an overweight, bedridden shadow of his former athletic self. The jousting accident he suffered in 1536 while celebrating Katharine of Aragon's death marked the decline of his health. Fistulas on his legs exuded an unbearable putrid odour and required changes of dressing several times a day. Immobilised by these "worst legs in the world", the King tried to remain active, but he was often moved from chamber to chamber by an indoor litter.[19]

In anticipation of his imminent death, Henry VIII composed his last will. This document largely dealt with the political situation after his demise and defined Henry's wishes for a Regency Council that would rule during his son's minority. But the King did not forget about his two daughters. Both Mary and Elizabeth each were to receive £3,000 "to live on" in "money, plate, jewels and household stuff".[20] They were still only "ladies" and not princesses, but their position as sisters to the new King was strong.

Henry VIII's death had a deep impact on the lives of his daughters. Within weeks of the King's passing, the fourteen-year-old Elizabeth received a proposal of marriage from Thomas Seymour, brother of the late Queen Jane. Henry VIII's last will stipulated that anyone who wanted to marry his daughters should seek the approval of the Privy Council first, but Elizabeth made it clear that she was not interested in marrying at this stage in her life nor so soon after her royal father's death. In an eloquent reply to Thomas Seymour's proposal, Elizabeth wrote:

"I confess to you that your letter, all elegant as it is, has very much surprised me; for, besides that neither my age nor my inclination allows me to think of marriage, I never could have believed that anyone would have spoken to me of nuptials, at a time when I ought to think of nothing but sorrow for the death of my father. And to him I owe so much that I must have two years at least to mourn for his loss."[21]

Seymour was not prepared to wait that long for Elizabeth, and he started courting her stepmother, the Dowager Queen Katherine Parr. Aged thirty-five, Katherine was torn between duty and her own desires. After four marriages—her husbands were either mentally incapacitated or past their prime—she still had no offspring, although she yearned to have a child of her own. As a royal widow, she was expected to wait at least two years before marrying again, but she was not getting any younger, and Thomas urged her "to change the two years into two months". Before she agreed, Katherine emphasised that her decision did not proceed from "any sudden motion or passion" because she had been in love with Thomas before King Henry started courting her in 1543.[22]

The couple married in great secrecy in the spring of 1547, causing a scandal at court and outraging many, including Mary and Elizabeth. The remarriage of royal widows was a delicate matter, and Katherine needed the permission of the Privy Council, headed by the Lord Protector, Edward Seymour, Katherine's brother-in-law. Yet the Lord Protector refused to allow the marriage to take place out of respect for the late King, but also because he was envious of his younger brother marrying a woman of higher social standing than his own wife. When Thomas and Katherine realised that their marriage plans were highly unpopular and were damaging the Dowager Queen's reputation, they decided to appeal to Mary. Could she, they wondered, use her influence with the Lord Protector and King Edward VI to help them facilitate their nuptials?

Mary was stunned when Thomas Seymour revealed that he wanted to marry Katherine Parr. She refused to be "a meddler in this matter, considering whose wife Her Grace was of late". If, Mary added, Katherine favoured his matrimonial suit, her recommendation would "do you but small pleasure". The wording of Mary's eloquent epistle suggests that she hoped that Katherine would not hurry into a new marriage; "if the remembrance of the King's majesty, my father ... will not suffer her to grant your suit, I am nothing able to persuade her to forget the loss of him, who is as yet very ripe in mine own remembrance".[23]

The news of their unsanctioned marriage reached court in July 1547. Mary remained outwardly calm, but inside she was seething with anger. As a dutiful daughter, she wore black for mourning and refused to dine in public when at court. When the imperial ambassador Van der Delft visited her before she left for her estates in the North, she asked him his opinion of Katherine Parr's hasty remarriage. The ambassador condemned the Dowager Queen for having been "content to forget the honour she had enjoyed from the late King".[24] "I was also the more pleased at the marriage" the ambassador continued, "because it meant that she herself [Mary] had thus escaped an alliance with the personage in question, for which, according to common report, she was at one time designated". It was true: King Edward VI had once suggested that if Thomas Seymour were to marry anyone, he should marry Mary to convert her to Protestantism. Mary's reaction to the rumours of her marriage to Seymour was telling and revealed the depth of her contempt for Katherine Parr:

"She laughed at this, saying that she had never spoken to him [Thomas Seymour] in her life, and had only seen him once; and she took in very good part my remark that, but for the perfect confidence I had in her prudence and discretion I should have come to her and have begged her to bear in mind her great descent and the respect due to her person, which should never tolerate such a degradation."[25]

Mary took it upon herself to inform Elizabeth of their stepmother's folly. Writing back, Elizabeth could scarcely contain her emotions. "I cannot express to you", she wrote, "how much affliction I suffered when I was first informed of this marriage". She elaborated further:

"You are very right in saying, in your most acceptable letters, which you have done me the honour of writing to me, that, in our interests being common, the just grief we feel in seeing the ashes, or rather the scarcely cold body of the King, our father, so shamefully dishonoured by the Queen, our stepmother, ought to be common to us also."

The sisters wondered what to do next. As a younger sibling, Elizabeth was obliged by custom to visit her stepmother from time to time, but she wanted Mary to know that she was not in a hurry to do so:

"With regard to the returning of visits, I do not see that you, who are elder, are obliged to this; but the position in which I stand obliges me to take other measures; the Queen having shown me so great affection, and done me so many kind offices, that I must use much tact in manoeuvring with her, for fear of appearing ungrateful for her benefits. I shall not, however, be in any hurry to visit her, lest I should be charged with approving what I ought to censure."[26]

Unfortunately for Elizabeth's resolve, she soon learned that the King had decided she should join Katherine Parr's household. At thirteen, she was deemed too young to have an establishment of her own, and the Dowager Queen yearned to have Elizabeth with her. But instead of a safe haven, Katherine Parr's household became the stage of one of the most dramatic events of Elizabeth's life.

Thomas Seymour, who moved in with Katherine Parr shortly after their wedding, was not immune to Elizabeth's beauty and started acting seductively towards her. He made it his habit to visit Elizabeth's bedchamber before she was out of bed, wishing her "good morrow and ask how she did, or strike her upon the back". If he found her still in bed, Seymour would draw back the bed curtains, bid her "good morrow" and "make as though he would come at her". Seymour often came to Elizabeth's bedchamber dressed only in his nightgown, "bare legged and in his slippers", but he usually found her reading a book. It seems as though Elizabeth made it her habit to rise early in order to be dressed before Seymour's visitation.[27]

When Elizabeth's governess informed Katherine Parr of Seymour's behaviour, the Dowager Queen made light of the accusations. On one occasion, however, she caught Thomas cradling Elizabeth in his arms and decided to send her stepdaughter away. The two never saw each other again since Katherine died as a result of childbed fever on 5 September 1548.

After the Dowager Queen's death, Thomas Seymour revived his plans for marrying Elizabeth, but the Lord Protector warned him that if Thomas went after Elizabeth, he would "clamp him in the Tower".[28] Thomas, always envious of his elder brother's influence, began plotting against him, trying to convince Edward VI to act independently of the Lord Protector. Edward Seymour quickly grasped what was going on and sent Thomas to the Tower. Elizabeth was interrogated as to her relationship with Thomas, and soon rumours started circulating at court that she was expecting his child—rumours that Elizabeth fiercely denied. Thomas Seymour was executed on 20 March 1549. Elizabeth survived the scandal that almost tarnished her reputation, but she would never again allow any man to be so bold towards her.

NOTES

[1] Agnes Strickland, *The Queens of England and Their Times*, Volume 1, p. 475.
[2] Agnes Strickland, *Lives of the Queens of England*, Volume 4-5, p. 136.
[3] *Calendar of State Papers, Spain,* Volume 5 Part 2, n. 72.
[4] Henry Clifford, *The Life of Jane Dormer, Duchess of Feria*, p. 80.
[5] *Letters and Papers, Henry VIII,* Volume 11, n. 860.
[6] *Letters and Papers, Henry VIII,* Volume 10, n. 1187.
[7] Ibid., n. 1186.
[8] Ibid., n. 1187.
[9] Ibid., Volume 12 Part 2, n. 911.
[10] Frederick Madden, *Privy Purse Expenses of the Princess Mary*, pp. 44, 45.
[11] M.A.Sharp Hume (ed.), *Chronicle of King Henry VIII (The Spanish Chronicle)*, p. 73.
[12] *Letters and Papers, Foreign and Domestic, Henry VIII,* Volume 13 Part 1, n. 402.
[13] Ibid., n. 647.
[14] Ibid., n. 931.
[15] Sylvia Barbara Soberton, *Great Ladies*, p. 112.
[16] *Letters and Papers, Henry VIII,* Volume 21 Part 1, n. 969.
[17] Herbert Norris, *Tudor Costume and Fashion*, p. 363.
[18] *Calendar of State Papers, Spain,* Volume 5 Part 2, n. 9.
[19] *Letters and Papers, Henry VIII,* Volume 19 Part 1, n. 529.
[20] J. L., McIntosh, *From Heads of Household to Heads of State*, p. 36.
[21] M. A. Everett Wood, *Letters of Royal and Illustrious Ladies of Great Britain*, Volume 3, p. 192.
[22] Janel Mueller, *Katherine Parr: Complete Works and Correspondence*, pp. 131, 135.
[23] Ibid., p. 146.
[24] *Calendar of State Papers, Spain,* Volume 9: 10 July 1547.
[25] Ibid.
[26] M. A. Everett Wood, *Letters of Royal and Illustrious Ladies of Great Britain*, Volume 3, p. 193-4.
[27] *A Collection of State Papers, 1542-1570*, p. 99.
[28] Leanda de Lisle, *The Sisters Who Would be Queen*, p. 49.

Chapter 5: "Your loving sister, Elizabeth"

Both Mary and Elizabeth enjoyed a warm relationship with their half brother, King Edward VI, but it was Elizabeth to whom the young sovereign was closest. Elizabeth's reputation had not been shattered by Thomas Seymour's execution and the revelations of his romantic intentions towards her. She was still highly regarded by the King, whose affection towards her was clear to all. "The Lady Elizabeth, sister to the King, arrived at court the other day, was received with great pomp and triumph, and is continually with the King", wrote the imperial ambassador François van der Delft in December 1549.[1]

Elizabeth, only four years older than Edward VI and brought up as a Protestant like him, had more in common with the King than Mary. At thirty-three, Mary was much older than both of her half siblings, and the religious differences between them soon became a bone of contention. Van der Delft noticed that the King and his councillors cherished a higher opinion of Elizabeth because she conformed to religious changes and accepted the new regime without protest. Mary, on the other hand, disapproved of Edward VI's religious views and the changes daily occurring in England.

Edward ascended the throne at the tender age of nine in January 1547, but he was too young to rule in his own right, and Henry VIII had made necessary provisions for his son's guidance and government in the last weeks of his life. He designated that sixteen executors of his last will would constitute a Council of Regency with twelve other advisors. The old King made it luminously clear that he wanted decisions to be taken by a majority vote and that there would be no one individual who would have pre-eminence over the others. Yet Henry VIII's last will was thwarted immediately after his death. The young King's maternal uncle, Edward Seymour, became Lord Protector of England and the Duke of Somerset. It was he who made all of the important decisions in the country, and Mary saw her half brother as a mere puppet in the Lord Protector's hands. By early 1550, the Lord Protector had lost his position, and another man, John Dudley—"the most unstable man in England" in Mary's view—took his place as the leading peer of Edward VI's regime.[2]

When Mary received an invitation to attend Christmas festivities in 1549 with Edward and Elizabeth, she pleaded ill health and politely declined. She later confided to the imperial ambassador Van der Delft that she knew that if she went to court for Christmas, a clash over religious matters with her half brother would be inevitable:

"They wished me to be at court so that I could not get the [Catholic] Mass celebrated for me, and that the King might take me with him to hear their sermons and Masses. I would not find myself in such a place for anything in the world. I will choose a more convenient time to go and pay my duty to the King, when I need not lodge at Court, for I have my own establishment in London. I shall stay four or five days only, and avoid entering into argument with the King, my brother, who, as I hear, is beginning to debate the question of religion and oppose ours, as he is being taught to do."[3]

Yet Mary could not avoid confrontation and arrived to court for Christmas in 1550 for a belated family reunion. The meeting was a disaster. Edward tried to convince Mary that, as his subject, she should be a good example to others, conform and forsake Catholicism. Mary always took an attack on her faith as an attack on herself and told Edward that, at thirteen, he was too young to make up his own mind about religion. A quarrel ensued between the two, and both were reduced to tears. This was not an isolated example of the strained relations between the siblings. Edward's entire reign was difficult for Mary since the young King insisted that, as the Head of the Anglican Church established by his father, he should and would change his half sister's religious views. But in this respect he did not understand Mary. Religion was her refuge, and she would often say that she was prepared to die for it. The fervent wish of becoming a martyr for the Catholic religion was something that had been instilled in Mary by her late mother; she once remarked that she would rather "lay her head on a block and suffer death" than forsake Catholicism.[4] Yet despite this bold assertion, at a point when tensions became unbearable for her frayed nerves, Mary contemplated escaping from England. Perhaps she was not willing to become a martyr after all. She stayed only because the imperial ambassador convinced her that if she ran away and her brother died childless, she would find it difficult to return and claim the throne. In the end, Mary won the dispute with Edward after invoking her powerful European connections; her cousin Charles V threatened England with war if Mary was not allowed the freedom of confession.

Mary could not but notice that Elizabeth was made much of at court. "A few days ago the Lady Elizabeth, sister of the King, came to London with a great suite of gentlemen and ladies, escorted by one hundred of the King's horse", reported the imperial ambassador in January 1551. "She was most honourably received by the Council, who acted thus in order to show the people how much glory belongs to her who has embraced the new religion and is become a very great lady".[5]

By now, Elizabeth was eighteen and a very great lady indeed. Like Mary, she ran her own royal household, moving between her country manors of Hatfield, Hunsdon and Ashridge, and had her own body of servants and retainers. She also was in full possession of her share of goods from Henry VIII's inventory. The late King stipulated that both of his daughters were free to choose whatever items they pleased from his vast collection of clothes, jewels, plate and furnishings. Elizabeth picked items that underlined her royal connections when her household was established in December 1548. Most notable among them were chairs with Henry VIII's coat of arms covered with fabrics of cloth of gold and crimson velvet. The canopies that hung over them were made of rich materials such as taffeta, cloth of silver and silk in white and crimson.

After Edward Seymour's execution on 22 January 1552, John Dudley emerged as the political force behind the throne. Elizabeth established a close link with the Dudleys, especially with one of John's sons, Robert, whom she had known since she was eight years old. John Dudley was never a popular figure, and in November 1550 the imperial ambassador reported that he heard "from a safe source" that John was "about to cast off his wife and marry my Lady Elizabeth, daughter of the late King, with whom he is said to have had several secret and intimate personal communications; and by these means he will aspire to the crown". This "safe source" may have been none other than Mary, who was the imperial ambassador's chief informant and bore small love for both Dudley and her half sister, whom she firmly believed was the product of Anne Boleyn's extramarital affair with one of her lovers.[6] These rumours, however, were far from the truth since Dudley and his wife were very close, and it is unlikely that he had ever contemplated discarding her.

During the majority of Edward's short reign, Mary and Elizabeth remained in touch mostly through letters. There's only one surviving epistle from this period, written by Elizabeth to Mary in October 1552. Addressing the letter to "my well-beloved sister Mary", Elizabeth expressed sadness at the state of her half sister's fragile health: "As to hear of your sickness is unpleasant to me, so it is nothing fearful, for that I understand it is your old guest that is wont oft to visit you, whose coming, though it be oft, yet it is never welcome." Elizabeth was referring to Mary's notoriously unstable health and a host of illnesses she suffered from, such as irregular menstruations, frequent headaches and catarrhs, as well as a recurrent affliction that always occurred "at the fall of the leaf". The phrase suggests that this recurrent illness happened during autumn. Depression has a tendency to develop in the autumn; it is then known as seasonal affective disorder. Since Mary was prone to suffer her "old guest" precisely "at the fall of the leaf", she certainly suffered from this seasonal depression that today is recognised as part of major depressive disorder.

It is clear from Elizabeth's letter that she courted Mary's favour and that the two exchanged correspondence regularly: "Good sister, though I have good cause to thank you for your oft sending to me, yet I have more occasion to render you my hearty thanks for your gentle writing, which how painful it is to you, I may well guess by myself."[7] Little did they both know that their relationship was soon to be tested by an unpredictable twist of fate.

NOTES

[1] *Calendar of State Papers, Spain,* Volume 9, 1547-1549, 19 December 1549.
[2] *Calendar of State Papers, Spain,* Volume 10, 1547-1549, 14 January 1549.
[3] Ibid.
[4] Sir Henry Ellis, *Original Letters, Illustrative of English History: To 1586,* p. 180.
[5] *Calendar of State Papers, Spain,* Volume 10, 1547-1549, 19 January 1549.
[6] Ibid., n. 4 January 1550.
[7] *Elizabeth I: Collected Works,* ed. Leah S. Marcus, Janel Mueller, Mary Beth Rose, pp. 37-8.

Chapter 6:
"Completely reconciled"

Four years into Edward VI's reign, Mary's and Elizabeth's positions as his heiresses appeared strong. In the autumn of 1551, as it became clear that Marie de Guise, Dowager Queen of Scotland, would land in England on her way home from France, Edward sent "letters to the Lady Mary and the Lady Elizabeth signifying unto them the arrival of the Dowager Queen of Scotland at Portsmouth, and her coming to the King's presence, and passage through the realm".[1] To honour Mary as heiress to his throne, Edward VI invited her to play the role of hostess during the Dowager Queen's reception, but Mary feared that the King might detain her at court or worse, "talk to her about the new religion and urge her to adopt it", and politely declined the offer, citing her ill health.[2] Instead of Mary, the wives of the leading political figures of Edward VI's regime entertained Marie de Guise on English soil. Oddly, Elizabeth, Edward's favourite sister, also did not appear at the Dowager Queen's reception.

In early 1553, Edward VI fell sick, and his condition was serious enough for his councillors to worry about the succession. Mary was Edward's heiress, but she was a Catholic, and her accession would inevitably destroy the Edwardian Reformation. In 1552, the Second Book of Common Prayer was introduced, and the altars were stripped from churches throughout the country.

Mary, who vehemently fought for her right to hold on to her Catholic beliefs, was allowed to hear Mass "privately in her house, without admitting of any strangers [foreigners]" and visited court in February 1553. Mary's arrival to London was a great spectacle and attracted attention. She was accompanied through the streets of the capital by "a great number of lords and knights, and all the great ladies". Among the women who greeted her were Frances Grey, Duchess of Suffolk, Elisabeth Parr, Marchioness of Northampton, and Jane Dudley, Duchess of Northumberland.[3] The King's sister was received with great honors, "as if she had been Queen of England". Mary was received in Edward VI's bedchamber since he was ill and confined to bed. Edward entertained her with "small talk", carefully avoiding the subject of religion that had divided them during the previous years.[4] The visit underlined Mary's importance as Edward's successor. But only two months later, the King changed his mind and cut both of his sisters from the succession.

Edward's health failed to improve. In late April 1553, the imperial ambassador Jehan Scheyfve observed that the sixteen-year-old King was "undoubtedly becoming weaker as time passes". "The matter he ejects from his mouth is sometimes coloured a greenish yellow and black, sometimes pink, like the colour of blood", Scheyfve reported and added that the King's physicians were perplexed and did not know what to make of his symptoms. It soon became apparent that Edward VI was dying.

The King's mind turned to the succession. Despite his youth, Edward was zealously dedicated to religious reform. According to the terms of his father's 1544 Act of Succession, confirmed by Henry VIII's last will of 1547, Edward's elder half sister, Mary, stood to inherit the crown. Everyone in England knew that, and many assumed that Mary would soon become Queen. Edward was horrified by the prospect of Mary inheriting his kingdom because he knew she would bring Catholicism back and undo all his reforms. "I am convinced that my sister Mary would provoke great disturbances after I have left this life", he told his councillors, adding that he planned to disinherit both Mary and Elizabeth.[5] Edward reasoned that he had solid grounds to do so since it was Henry VIII himself who annulled his marriages to Katharine of Aragon and Anne Boleyn, illegitimating their daughters in the process:

> "For indeed my sister Mary was the daughter of the King by Katharine the Spaniard, who before she was married to my worthy father had been espoused to Arthur, my father's elder brother, and was therefore for this reason divorced from my father. But it was the fate of Elizabeth, my other sister, to have Anne Boleyn for a mother; this woman was indeed not only cast off by my father because she was more inclined to couple with a number of courtiers rather than reverencing her husband, so mighty a King, but also paid the penalty with her head—a greater proof of guilt. Thus in our judgment they will be undeservedly considered as being numbered among the heirs of the King our beloved father."[6]

The exclusion of Mary seemed rational—Edward was always trying to convert her, and he was not personally attached to her. The exclusion of Elizabeth seemed suspicious to most people who knew how close the young King was to his "Sweet Sister Temperance", as he affectionately referred to her. The two often exchanged correspondence, and at some point the King ordered Elizabeth's portrait. She was a frequent guest at his court and basked in his attention. Furthermore, she was of the same religious conviction as Edward. Following the precedent set in his father's last will, Edward VI also bypassed the heirs of Henry VIII's elder sister, Margaret Tudor, Queen of Scots. This left the heirs of Edward's junior aunt, Mary Tudor, Dowager Queen of France, and her husband, Charles Brandon, Duke of Suffolk.

With both of his sisters out of the way, the kingdom was to be inherited by the male offspring of his first cousin, Frances Grey, Duchess of Suffolk. If she would have no sons, then the crown was to pass to the sons of Jane, Katherine or Mary Grey, Frances's daughters. The Greys had close ties to the royal family. Frances Grey, née Brandon, was the daughter of Mary Tudor, Henry VIII's younger sister, and Charles Brandon, Duke of Suffolk. In 1533, she married Henry Grey, Marquess of Dorset, the great-grandson of Elizabeth Woodville and her first husband, John Grey of Groby. In 1551, Henry Grey was created Duke of Suffolk after the male line of the Brandon Dukes of Suffolk became extinct.

Frances and Henry had three daughters: Jane, Katherine and Mary. Jane Grey, the eldest, was their pride and joy. She was raised in the teachings of the New Religion and was more pious than her young age merited. She was also exceptionally talented and preferred reading Greek philosophers to hunting, as her tutor Roger Ascham later recorded in his memoirs. Ascham believed that Jane was naturally inclined to read great classical philosophers because she derived her birth "both on your father's side and on your mother's from kings and queens".[7]

In the spring of 1553, Edward VI drew up his "devise for the succession". "For the lack of issue male of my body", the frail King bequeathed his kingdom "to the issue male coming of the issue female, as I have after declared. To the Lady Frances's heirs males, if she have any; for lack of such issue before my death, to the Lady Jane's heirs males; to the Lady Katherine's heirs males; to the Lady Mary's heirs males; to the heirs males of the daughters which she [Frances Grey] shall have hereafter . . ."[8] The devise also specified that if these women failed to produce male heirs, the crown was to pass on to the male offspring of Margaret Clifford, Frances's niece.[9]

The early draft of the King's devise makes it clear that he did not originally plan to be succeeded by a female. It was only after he realised that he would die sooner than any male heir was born to his kinswomen that he decided for a radical change of the document. "If I die without issue and there be none heir male", Edward reiterated once again, "then the Lady Frances to be Governess Regent . . . until some heir male be born, and then the mother of that child to be Governess". The situation envisaged by the dying King was politically dangerous, and he soon changed his devise for the last time. He was now convinced that Lady Jane Grey was eminently suitable to become his successor since she was of royal descent and Protestant faith. The phrase "Lady Jane's heirs males" was altered to "Lady Jane *and her* heirs male".[10] With the addition of just two short words, Jane Grey became heiress to the throne.

Edward VI died on 6 July 1553, but his death was kept in strict secrecy. Four days later, on 10 July, Lady Jane Grey was proclaimed Queen of England. An obscure figure, Lady Jane failed to elicit loyalty in the hearts of her fellow countrymen, who firmly believed that she was being used as a figurehead by John Dudley, Duke of Northumberland, her father-in-law. When a teenaged boy, Gilbert Potter, shouted out that Mary was the rightful Queen, he was arrested and his ears were nailed to a pillory and cut off as punishment.

Mary's chance to regain her throne looked bleak—she was isolated in East Anglia and had no funds and no soldiers. Her chances, in the French ambassadors' opinion, were "well-nigh impossible".[11] But Mary had something that others didn't suspect—her strong will, determination and a firm belief that she was chosen by God. Mary also firmly believed that Lady Jane Grey, her second cousin, was a puppet in Northumberland's hands and didn't consider her as dangerous. She also didn't believe that Edward VI's last will was his own idea—he too, in her view, was Northumberland's pawn.

The memory of Henry VIII still loomed large, and Mary decided to invoke her late father's last will to highlight her right to the throne. Writing to Jane Grey's Council from Kenninghall Castle in the north of England, Mary adopted the royal "we" and referred to Henry VIII's last will that, unlike her brother's, was enshrined in parliamentary statutes: "You know, the realm and the whole world knoweth, the rolls and record appear by the authority of the King our said father, and the King our said brother, and the subjects of this realm; so that we verily trust that there is no good true subject, that is, can, or would, pretend to be ignorant thereof."[12]

But if Mary thought this letter would gain her supporters, she was mistaken. The councillors replied referring to Mary as "lady" rather than "Queen" and reminded her that her father had proclaimed her illegitimate by an Act of Parliament. Northumberland was even fiercer in his defiance of Mary's right to the throne, writing circulars sent to justices of the peace, ordering them to "assist us in our rightful possession of this Kingdom and to extirp to disturb, repel and resist the fained [feigned] and untrue claim of the Lady Mary bastard". There was to be a battle for the throne. Lady Jane Grey's father was to lead an army against Mary with the aim of capturing and perhaps even killing her, but Jane, sensibly enough, forbade her father to go and "with weeping tears" requested the Council to allow him to stay with her in the Tower.[13] Instead, the Duke of Northumberland went at the head of the army. Mary's situation now looked hopeless, and even her beloved kinsman Charles V, Holy Roman Emperor, believed that Mary's "chances of coming to the throne are very slight".[14] He didn't lift a finger to help her.

But Mary had supporters in England and rallied them to her cause while staying in the north. On 12 July 1553, she moved from Kenninghall to Framlingham Castle in Suffolk with the aim of defending her claim to the throne. Framlingham was a large structure with a curtain wall with thirteen mural towers to defend the centre of the castle. The castle's military history had long been forgotten, however, since the last siege occurred in 1216. The castle had recently served as a luxurious residence of the Howard family and had devolved upon Mary after the third Duke of Norfolk's arrest in 1547. Mary's arrival to Framlingham was greeted by "a great concourse of people", and when her flag was triumphantly unfurled over the gate tower, it looked like another war for succession was to be fought on English soil.[15]

In the end, there was no battle, and Mary took possession of the crown without one drop of blood being shed. Without Northumberland's commanding presence at her side, support for Lady Jane Grey began to crumble. Councillors, who gathered around Jane in the Tower when she entered there on 10 July 1553, started defecting. Mary was proclaimed queen on 19 July 1553.

Elizabeth's reaction to these events remains unknown, but she must have followed them closely because, when news spread that Mary had won the throne, she immediately sent her a congratulatory letter and asked "what dress she desires to see her when she goes to salute her: whether her garb shall be mourning or not".[16] The sisters met on 29 July 1553 when Elizabeth arrived at Somerset Place to take part in Mary's grand entry into London. Elizabeth came to court "with a goodly company of mounted men", all dressed in Tudor colours of green and white. The Queen welcomed her with "great warmth" and kissed all of her ladies-in-waiting as a mark of high esteem. On 3 August 1553, Queen Mary made her entry into the capital. It was a grand spectacle designed to impress the masses who greeted Mary's accession with elation.

Besides "the nobility in great numbers", the Queen was escorted by "over a thousand men-at-arms, mounted and on foot... in their accoutrements of war, besides her body-guard". Mary herself was mounted on a richly caparisoned horse. "She was dressed in violet velvet, her skirts and sleeves embroidered in gold; her face is more than middling-fair; her equipage was regal", enthused the Spanish ambassador.[17] Behind the Queen rode Sir Anthony Browne, her Master of the Horse, leading a spare palfrey. Elizabeth, as the Queen's sister and heiress, rode behind, accompanied by Elizabeth Howard, Duchess of Norfolk, and Gertrude Courtenay, Marchioness of Exeter. Both of these women were Elizabeth's kin, but neither of them had warm feelings for her since they were her late mother's implacable enemies. A "flock" of 180 "peeresses, gentlewomen and ladies-in-waiting, never before seen in such numbers", followed after them.[18]

The cavalcade wound its way towards London, stopping by at St Botolph's Church, where a large scaffold was erected. About one hundred "poor children" of the Christ's Hospital, recently founded by the late Edward VI, stood on the scaffold. One of the children stepped forward, knelt down and delivered an oration in Latin, praising the new Queen and praying "that she might take them under her care".[19] The anonymous author of *Queen Jane's Chronicle* reported with disapproval that Mary "said nothing to them", but the Spanish ambassador, impressed by the sight, reported that "they were given to the Queen to nourish and care for them, the eldest not being over twelve or fourteen".[20]

The cavalcade proceeded through Aldgate, "which was richly hanged with arras and set with streamers", through Leaden Hall, Grace Church Street, Fenchurch Street, down the Mark Lane "and so to the Tower". When she entered the fortress, Mary freed the prisoners of previous political systems: Thomas Howard, Duke of Norfolk; Stephen Gardiner, Bishop of Winchester; Anne Seymour, Duchess of Somerset; and Edward Courtenay, son of the executed Marquis of Exeter.

Despite the fact that Lady Jane Grey had usurped her throne, Queen Mary planned no punishment for her young kinswoman. "Her conscience, she said, would not permit her to have her put to death", she revealed to the Spanish ambassador. Mary perceived Jane as a puppet in the Duke of Northumberland's hands. Her view was further strengthened by a self-abasing letter Jane wrote to Mary in the aftermath of Mary's accession. Jane presented her own version of events, depicting herself as victim of Northumberland's ambition. She wrote that she never really wanted to occupy Mary's throne but was forced to do so by Northumberland and his crew. "For although I took upon me that of which I was unworthy, yet no one can say that I ever sought to obtain it for myself, nor ever solaced myself therein, nor accepted it willingly", she recalled.[21] This was enough to convince Queen Mary that Jane was an unwilling participant in Northumberland's intrigue.

Lady Jane Grey's usurpation planted fear and suspicion in the Queen's mind. Jane was a Tudor, but she was unknown to the populace and her accession had been met with disapproval. The Queen's sister, on the other hand, was a popular figure and had been brought up under close public scrutiny, just as Mary had been. Elizabeth, Mary feared, might become a figurehead for possible rebellions. Charles V's ambassadors, Mary's closest foreign allies, tried to capitalise on the Queen's fears, pointing out that

Elizabeth was "clever and sly" and could "out of ambition, or being persuaded thereto, conceive some dangerous design and put it to execution". Elizabeth had no designs upon Mary's crown, but she was a powerful allurement for malcontents. Despite harbouring suspicions as to Elizabeth's loyalty, Mary told the Imperial ambassadors that she planned to send her sister away from court after her coronation "and before setting the Lady Jane at liberty she would take the greatest possible care for the future".[22]

Whereas Mary intended to pardon Lady Jane, she was eager to punish John Dudley, Duke of Northumberland. His wife, who was arrested but soon released, made an attempt to plead with the Queen for his life, but Mary wouldn't see her. On 18 August 1553, Northumberland was tried and sentenced to death. To the astonishment of those who knew him, "the most unstable man in England", as Mary had dubbed him three years previously, converted to Catholicism, perhaps in the hope of the Queen sparing his life.[23] In a letter to the Earl of Arundel, Northumberland wrote that "a living dog is better than a dead lion" and begged Arundel to speak on his behalf with the Queen: "Oh, that it would please her good Grace to give me life! Yea, the life of a dog, if I might but live and kiss her feet, and spend both life and all in her honorable service." Mary would not

"Completely reconciled"

grant him "the life of a dog", and Northumberland's execution was carried out as scheduled on 22 August 1553.[24]

The Queen's coronation was still two months away, and Elizabeth stayed at court with Mary. She was horrified to discover that Catholic Masses were celebrated openly six or seven times a day and that her sister had stopped hiding her intentions of restoring England to the Church of Rome. The imperial ambassadors noted with some distaste that Elizabeth and Lady Anne of Cleves, the Tudor sisters' former stepmother, were not present during Catholic Masses. Pressure was mounting, and the Queen had no intention of allowing Elizabeth a free choice in the matter of religion. She was instigated by Stephen Gardiner, who had become Lord Chancellor shortly after his release from the Tower.

Gardiner started his brilliant court career under Henry VIII. In the 1520s and 1530s, he helped the King achieve his desired outcome during the annulment. He exchanged some cordial correspondence with Elizabeth's mother, Anne Boleyn, but England's split with Rome horrified him, and he became an implacable enemy of the Reformers. A brilliant statesman, Gardiner was later embroiled in factional power struggles during the last years of Henry VIII's reign and nearly destroyed the King's sixth wife, Katherine Parr, when he dared to accuse her of heresy. Excluded from the Regency Council by the King, Gardiner spent the entirety of Edward VI's reign in the Tower. Queen Mary, who applauded Gardiner for his zeal in weeding out heresy, had every reason to restore him to an honourable position and made him her Lord Chancellor. In July, he moved into Winchester Palace in Southwark, previously occupied by William Parr, Marquis of Northampton, and his wife, Elisabeth. The palace, refurbished by its previous owners, was a luxurious residence so much different from the bare walls Gardiner used to look at in the Tower each day for five years.

The new Lord Chancellor believed that Elizabeth, brought up in "the errors and convictions" of Protestant doctrine, should become Catholic since the prospect of a Protestant heiress succeeding to the throne after Mary horrified him and the Queen. During an audience he granted the imperial ambassadors in late August, Gardiner said that "persuasion has been used to try and correct the Lady Elizabeth and induce her to forsake error." Elizabeth proved receptive and promised the Queen that she would take part in a Catholic Mass on 8 September, the Feast of the Nativity of the Virgin Mary. "Events will prove whether she is doing so out of deceit, and the better to play the game of which she is suspected", the imperial ambassadors informed Charles V.[25]

The Nativity was one of the most important feasts in the Catholic calendar, and the Queen was especially attached to it since she was named after the Virgin Mary. Elizabeth was born on 7 September, the day preceding the feast, and Mary could not ask for a better date to humble her sister. But Elizabeth was cautious. Several days before the feast, she asked to see the Queen privately. "Perceiving that the Queen did not show her as kindly a countenance as she could wish, and judging and supposing that the reason of it was her obstinacy in error, she besought the Queen to grant her a private audience", the imperial ambassadors informed Charles V. Mary didn't agree at once, but she knew she had no other choice but to allow Elizabeth a private meeting. After all, Elizabeth had committed no crime. Two days later the sisters met "in a certain gallery where there was a door or half-door between the Queen and the Lady Elizabeth". The Queen was accompanied by "one of her ladies", most likely the trusted Susan Clarencius, who was always by her side during seemingly private audiences. Elizabeth came with one of her maids whose identity was not recorded.

When Elizabeth saw Mary, she knelt in front of her "on both knees", a sign of reverence and respect, and started weeping. She said that "she saw only too clearly that the Queen was not well-disposed towards her, and she knew of no other cause except religion". Instead of making excuses for herself and trying to argue over religious differences of their respective faiths, Elizabeth sought common ground. Unlike Mary, she "had never been taught the doctrine of the ancient religion". Could Mary send her books and a learned man to instruct her in the Catholic doctrine so that "she might know if her conscience would allow her to be persuaded"?

Mary had expected Elizabeth to mount a spirited defence of her Protestant convictions and was surprised by her sister's willingness to convert. She was "exceedingly glad to see her turn to such good resolves" and granted Elizabeth's request. The imperial ambassadors concluded that the Queen's sister "was converted and abjured her errors". To confirm her change of faith, Elizabeth went to Mass on 8 September 1553, but the way she did it planted suspicion in the Queen's mind yet again. Elizabeth tried to "excuse herself, saying she was ill, and complained loudly all the way to church that her stomach ached, wearing a suffering air". This was Elizabeth's way of sending a message to her followers: Yes, I converted. No, not willingly.

A key to Elizabeth's feelings at this time is glimpsed in a letter she wrote to her kinswoman Katherine Knollys. In September 1553, Protestants started leaving England in fear for their lives. Their decision was prompted by the fact that Queen Mary was a staunch opponent of "heresy" and had already sanctioned the arrests of leading Protestants: Thomas Cranmer, Archbishop of Canterbury, and Hugh Latimer, Bishop of Worcester.[26] The imperial ambassadors informed their master that:

"We have been warned that sundry foreign Lutherans who formerly inhabited this kingdom are withdrawing to your Majesty's Low Countries, being under accusation of causing scandal, and preaching false and forbidden doctrines. We cannot forbear from sending this information to your Majesty, so that you may take whatever steps seem best to you to protect your subjects."[27]

The Knollyses were among the exiles. Katherine, born in the early 1520s, was the daughter of Mary Boleyn and her first husband, William Carey. Since Mary Boleyn was Henry VIII's mistress, rumours spread that her two children were the King's and not her husband's. William Carey acknowledged Katherine and Henry Carey as his own, but they were possibly the King's bastards. Katherine especially resembled Henry VIII in looks, sharing his ruddy complexion and red hair. Elizabeth and Katherine were each other's best friends, the bond between them strengthened by their shared Boleyn blood. Elizabeth signed her letter to Katherine calling herself "cor rotto", broken-hearted. "Relieve your sorrow for your far journey with joy of your short return, and think this pilgrimage rather a proof of your friends, than a leaving of your country", Elizabeth urged.[28]

Elizabeth may have felt that she was betraying her faith and her friends, but she could not leave England. She was her father's daughter, heiress to the throne and the Queen's sister. Surely Mary would treat her with kindness? If Elizabeth hoped so, she was about to be sorely disappointed.

In late September, the Queen continued to show kindness to Elizabeth and selected several jewels for her sister from her own collection. Mary was torn in her feelings for Elizabeth, the little sister she resented at first but eventually grew to love. Mary was seventeen years older than Elizabeth—old enough to be her mother. Over the years she treated Elizabeth as a substitute for the child she never had and lavished her unfulfilled maternal affection on the young girl. But as Elizabeth matured into a young woman, she started resembling Anne Boleyn in appearance and, Mary thought, in behaviour as well. The resemblance was unmistakable. Elizabeth's long face with high cheekbones and dark eyes were eerily reminiscent of her mother's. She also had Anne Boleyn's swarthy complexion, willowy figure and well-shaped long hands. Similarities didn't end there. Anne was said to have had "a very good wit", a sparkling personality with an air of self-confidence often taken for haughtiness. The imperial ambassador Renard noticed a dangerous if similar quality about Elizabeth's character; she had "a power of enchantment" and was thus to be greatly feared.[29]

Renard heard that Elizabeth sought to strengthen her claim to the throne by marrying Edward Courtenay, another claimant. Courtenay had recently been released from the Tower, where he spent fifteen years. Unlike many other prisoners, Courtenay didn't commit any crime; his only fault was being the son of an executed traitor. His father was Henry Courtenay, Marquis of Exeter, Henry VIII's first cousin. In 1538, Exeter and his friends and family were accused of conspiring with the King's enemies and encouraging foreign powers (Charles V, allied with the pope) to invade England and dethrone the mad tyrant, as they referred to Henry VIII in private. Their real crime, though, was their connection to Reginald Pole, the English cardinal in exile who wrote a painfully honest tract addressed to Henry VIII entitled *Defence of the Unity of the Church*. Pole's *Defence*, published shortly after Anne Boleyn's execution, defined his views on papal authority and the King's succession and praised those who died for their refusal to accept Henry's supremacy over the Church of England.

The tract was highly personal in nature, and the King perceived it as an attack, not only on his religious and domestic policies but on his royal person. Henry had immediately conceived such hatred towards Reginald Pole that he decided to hunt him down and make him "eat his own heart".[30] Those connected to Reginald Pole were either executed in a stunning miscarriage of justice or imprisoned. Even Pole's elderly mother, Margaret, Countess of Salisbury, was dragged from her prison cell and executed by an inexperienced executioner who "hacked her head and shoulders to pieces".

The Exeter Conspiracy of 1538 consumed the lives of those whom Queen Mary loved and respected. Margaret

Pole was her beloved governess for years before she was dismissed in 1534; Henry Courtenay was among her and Katharine of Aragon's staunchest supporters, and Reginald Pole himself strongly condemned Henry VIII for bastardising Mary and excluding her from the succession in 1536. It was thus hardly surprising that after she became Queen, Mary summoned members of these conservative families to her court. Gertrude, the widowed Marchioness of Exeter, was summoned in the summer of 1553 and instantly became Mary's closest companion. She became Mary's bedfellow, sleeping in the same bedchamber as the Queen, a mark of the highest favour. She was deeply grateful to Mary for reinstating her and releasing her son from the Tower.

Elizabeth, on the other hand, had no reason to love or trust these people. Gertrude was one of her three godmothers, but she had been forced to accept this dubious honour so as "not to displease the King". She and her late husband were personal friends and vocal supporters of Katharine of Aragon, and Mary, and were prepared to risk Henry VIII's wrath. Gertrude hated Anne Boleyn as much as she loved Katharine of Aragon. Anne, a shrewd judge of character, dismissed the marchioness from Katharine's service in 1530, a move that Gertrude never forgave.

In the summer of 1533, Gertrude contacted Elizabeth Barton, the famous Nun of Kent, who was broadcasting anti-Boleyn prophecies. The nun was executed in 1534, but Gertrude escaped the consequences of coming into contact with her, although she never ceased to plot against Anne Boleyn. She was one of the main informants of the imperial ambassador Eustace Chapuys, appearing in disguise on his doorstep on occasion, and was among the people who groomed Jane Seymour to supplant Anne Boleyn. When Anne was executed, Gertrude finally felt that justice had been served. Briefly imprisoned but released, she languished in obscurity after her husband's execution in 1538 but remained in touch with Mary, who regularly sent her gifts of jewellery as tokens of affection.

Renard heard that Elizabeth "already has her eye on Courtenay as a possible husband, because she knows Courtenay's mother is always welcome with the Queen, and usually sleeps with her. This is very dangerous; and I foresee that Courtenay's friends, who include most of the nobility, are hatching some design that may later menace the Queen".[31] This was not true, as Elizabeth hated the idea of matrimony from her early childhood and was not interested in Courtenay, whom she barely knew. Plus, Courtenay was interested in the Queen herself, hoping to wear the crown matrimonial. He was dazzled by the attention he received from nobility as he was "courted and followed about by the whole Court".

Contrary to popular myth, the fifteen years Courtenay spent in the Tower did not dull his wits. He received an excellent education, and thus "his incarceration, his prison and confinement have not been grievous to him, but have been converted into liberty by his studiousness and taste for letters and science". Despite growing up away from court, the imperial ambassadors judged that there was "civility" in Courtenay, which they thought "must be deemed natural rather than acquired by the habit of society; and his bodily graces are in proportion to those of his mind". Queen Mary felt personally responsible for his well-being and heaped favour after favour upon him, restoring him to the earldom of Devon that had belonged to his grandmother, Katherine of York, on 3 September 1553. But despite "much talk here to the effect that he will be married to the Queen as he is of the blood royal", Mary had no intention of marrying Courtenay. Mary was preparing for her coronation while her ladies-in-waiting "talked of nothing else but marriage", wondering whom the Queen would choose, but no one dared suggest a name for fear of displeasing her. [32] Thus, Courtenay's open talk about his hopes of marrying the Queen angered Mary.

Mary's coronation was a lavish spectacle. The Queen spared no expense to impress her subjects, who embraced her as their sovereign lady with enthusiasm. The last Tudor queen who was crowned was Anne Boleyn twenty years earlier, and she had been six months pregnant at the time. Clothes and jewels Anne wore for that occasion were still stored in the Great Wardrobe, and Mary wore them at her hour of triumph.

Coronations in England were held on a Sunday and were the culmination of a three-day cycle of elaborately staged events, starting with the monarch's arrival at the Tower, a procession through the city of London to Westminster and the coronation and anointing. On the day preceding her coronation, the Queen was carried in an open litter covered with brocade from the Tower, where she had spent the previous night appointing Knights of the Bath, to Westminster Palace. She was accompanied by earls, lords, gentlemen, ambassadors and officers, "all dressed in rich garments". The Queen's litter was followed by two coaches. In the first one travelled Lady Elizabeth and Anne of Cleves, two of the highest-ranking peeresses in England. The second one carried "some of the ladies of the Court".

"Completely reconciled"

The next day Mary, dressed in crimson and with her hair spread over her shoulders, made her way to Westminster Abbey, where she was "twice anointed and crowned with three crowns" on a specially erected platform so that everyone could see her. Nobility of the realm paid their homage to Mary, swearing fealty and kissing her on the shoulder. An elaborate banquet followed, with the Queen seated on a marble chair laid out with brocade, resting her feet on cushions held by two of her ladies-in-waiting. Mary was the first woman in England to be crowned and anointed as Queen regnant rather than consort. In 1141, Empress Matilda, daughter of Henry I, claimed the throne after her father died without a legitimate male heir but was never crowned as queen in her own right, and her rule was challenged by her cousin Stephen of Blois. It was Matilda's son, Henry II, who became King after Stephen died without a son in 1154, and who proudly called himself Henry FitzEmpress, "son of the Empress". Like Matilda, Mary was the daughter of a king. Her gender did not preclude her from attaining the crown, and her accession was smooth despite Lady Jane Grey's usurpation. Mary herself probably never perceived her gender as an obstacle since she came from a long line of women who wielded power equal to men. Her maternal grandmother, Isabella of Castile, was a queen in her own right in Spain, and her first cousin, Mary of Hungary, served as Governor of the Habsburg Netherlands from 1531 to 1555, a task that she was very successful in accomplishing.

The Queen's coronation was a foreshadowing of religious changes she intended to introduce in the country. The "ceremonies and solemnities" proceeded according to "the old custom," and thus as a full Roman Mass rather than as Communion. The second Act of Uniformity in 1552 and the publication of the second Book of Common Prayer had replaced "Mass" with "Communion" and erased the word "sacrament", but the Queen didn't acknowledge any of this, returning to the Catholic rituals of her childhood. She was crowned by the staunchly Catholic Bishop of Winchester and not by the Protestant Archbishop of Canterbury, another indication that Catholicism was to be restored.[33]

Elizabeth was accorded a place of honour during the Queen's coronation, but this was soon to change. Mary firmly believed that her sister was a dissembler who harboured ambitions of toppling her from the throne. She also could not believe that Elizabeth converted so easily to Catholicism, a religion that she barely knew. In a private audience with Simon Renard, Mary said that "it would burden her conscience too heavily to allow Elizabeth to

"Completely reconciled"

succeed, for she only went to Mass out of hypocrisy, she had not a single servant or maid of honour who was not a heretic, she talked every day with heretics and lent an ear to all their evil designs, and it would be a disgrace to the kingdom to allow a bastard to succeed".[34] Mary already knew what she would do with her sister: Elizabeth was to be "declared a bastard, having been born during the lifetime of Queen Katharine, mother of the Queen". The upcoming opening of Parliament on 5 October 1553 provided an opportunity for Mary to debar Elizabeth from succession once and for all.[35]

Mary never forgave Henry VIII for setting her mother aside for Anne Boleyn. Although Anne was crowned with St Edward's crown, Mary never referred to her as Queen, using instead the title of Marchioness of Pembroke that Anne received in 1532. Now, when she had all the power, Mary was eager to rewrite history and restore her mother's good name. In 1536, Mary had signed a document, according to which she was a bastard and her parents' marriage was void. She was always ashamed of the day she signed that paper and saw herself as the one who would reverse Henry VIII's acts.

During her first Parliament summoned on 5 October 1553, Mary reinforced her sister's bastardy by proclaiming the legality of the marriage between Henry VIII and Katharine of Aragon. The Queen also repealed all the religious reforms of Edward VI's reign, reinstating Catholicism as England's main religion. From that point on, Mary radically changed her attitude towards Elizabeth, "for whereas until then she had shown her every mark of honour, especially by always placing her beside her when she appeared in public, so did she now by all her actions show that she held her in small account".[36]

Elizabeth's degradation was painfully obvious when the Queen decreed that her first cousins Margaret, Countess of Lennox, and Frances, Duchess of Suffolk, were to take precedence over her sister. In late October, Elizabeth took part in a banquet, during which she sat with the Countess of Lennox, but other noblewomen were careful not to talk too much to her for fear of displeasing the Queen. Elizabeth, wrote the French ambassador Antoine de Noailles, "is in so much disfavour that there is not one lady in this court who dares to visit her in her chamber, or even to speak to her without the permission of the Queen". Elizabeth tried to dissemble and "was so little dismayed by this, that every day she has had all the young gentlemen of the Court to visit her, and takes pains to talk with them, expecting (so I understand) to gain her end in a few days, which is, in short, that she may obtain her dismissal and go to her own house, where she lived formerly".[37] She felt ill at ease at her sister's court and wanted to be back at Hatfield before Christmas.

Mary made no secret about how much she loathed Elizabeth, telling Simon Renard and William Paget that she would not allow her sister to succeed after her "because of her heretical opinions, illegitimacy and characteristics in which she resembled her mother". Anne Boleyn, the Queen said, "had caused great trouble in the kingdom", and she feared Elizabeth "might do the same, and particularly that she would imitate her mother in being a French partisan".[38] To prevent Elizabeth from succeeding, Mary wanted to marry and beget an heir, but if she died without issue, she preferred her first cousin Margaret Douglas to be her heiress since Margaret was her childhood friend and a good Catholic.

Elizabeth feared she may not be allowed to leave court since she had enemies among the Queen's councillors and foreign diplomats. Simon Renard, the imperial ambassador, was especially malicious and hardened against her. He believed that "it would be well to have Elizabeth more carefully watched, or better yet to shut her up in the Tower".[39] Yet, as Paget warned the Queen, Elizabeth's disinheritance or imprisonment were too dangerous and could cause social unrest.

When Elizabeth asked Mary to allow her to leave court, the Queen hesitated. She believed that Elizabeth was embroiled in intrigues with the French ambassador and preferred to have Elizabeth close at hand to carefully observe her. On 30 November 1553, just as the sisters, accompanied by their ladies, went to Mass, someone called "Treason!" in a very loud voice. The Queen went ahead to the chapel, but Elizabeth "was so much perturbed that she could not compose her countenance, and to pass off her paleness made Dame Clarencius rub her stomach, saying that she was amazed that the Queen had not retired after such a warning, and that she was trembling for fear some outrage might be attempted against her person".[40]

By early December 1553, Mary granted her permission for Elizabeth to leave court. Before Elizabeth left, she was visited by William Paget and the Earl of Arundel, who "warned her that if she refused to follow the path of duty and persisted in concerning herself with French and heretical conspiracies, she would bitterly repent it". Elizabeth knew that their message was issued by the Queen and replied that "regarding religion it was not timidity or hypocrisy which made her change, but rather her conscience and affection, and she would prove this by taking good churchmen with her and would send away any of her servants who were suspected, and, in short, do all in her power to win the Queen's approval". She also denied that she had any dealings with the French.

Simon Renard reported that Elizabeth "took a friendly leave of the Queen" and Mary "dissembled very well", presenting her sister with "a very beautiful sable wrap".[41] Elizabeth begged Mary "not to put faith in bad reports of her without hearing her defence, so that she might have an opportunity of proving her innocence, for these stories were merely lies on the part of those who desired her ruin". Mary smiled and nodded politely, deceiving the French ambassador into thinking that the sisters "were completely reconciled".[42] Privately, however, Mary was incandescent with rage. "I had much trouble in persuading the Queen to dissemble, for she still resents the injuries inflicted on Queen Katharine, her lady mother, by the machinations of Anne Boleyn, mother of Elizabeth, and recalls trouble and unpleasantness before and since her accession, unrest and disagreeable occurrences to which

Elizabeth has given rise", wrote Renard.[43] In other words, Mary was still living in the past. If only she could marry and produce an heir who would take Elizabeth's place in the line of succession. She was becoming obsessed with the idea of demoting Elizabeth, and since she was already in her late thirties, she needed to marry as quickly as possible.

NOTES

[1] *Acts of the Privy Council of England Volume 3, 1550-1552*, p. 397.
[2] *Calendar of State Papers, Spain*, Volume 10, 1550-1552, 31 October 1551.
[3] *The Diary of Henry Machyn*, p. 30.
[4] *Calendar of State Papers, Spain*, Volume 11, 1553, 17 February 1553.
[5] Anna Whitelock, *Mary Tudor: England's First Queen*, p. 139.
[6] Ibid., p. 163.
[7] Roger Ascham, *The Whole Works of Roger Ascham*, Volume I, p. 239.
[8] *The Honourable Society of the Inner Temple*: Edward VI's "My devise for the succession", Inner Temple Library, Petyt MS 538.47, f. 317.
[9] She was the daughter of Eleanor Clifford, née Brandon, Duchess of Cumberland, who died in 1547.
[10] Edward VI's "My devise for the succession", op.cit.
[11] Anna Whitelock, *Mary Tudor: England's First Queen*, p. 167.
[12] Ibid., p. 168.
[13] Ibid., p. 169.
[14] *Calendar of State Papers, Spain*, Volume 11, 10 July 1553.
[15] Anna Whitelock, *Mary Tudor: England's First Queen*, p. 171..
[16] *Calendar of State Papers, Spain*, Volume 11, 1553, 22 July 1553.
[17] Ibid., 6 August 1553.
[18] Charles Wriothesley, *Wriothesley's Chronicle*, Volume 2, p. 93.
[19] *Calendar of State Papers, Spain*, Volume 11, 6 August 1553.
[20] *The Chronicle of Queen Jane and the First Year of Queen Mary*, pp. 14, 15.
[21] *Writings of Edward the Sixth, William Hugh, Queen Catherine Parr, Anne Askew, Lady Jane Grey, Hamilton, and Balnaves*, p. 29.
[22] *Calendar of State Papers, Spain*, Volume 11, 16 August 1553.

[23] Ibid., Volume 10, 14 January 1550.
[24] D. M. Loades, *John Dudley, Duke of Northumberland, 1504-1553*, p. 269.
[25] *Calendar of State Papers, Spain,* Volume 11, 9 September 1553.
[26] Charles Wriothesley, *Wriothesley's Chronicle*, Volume 2, p. 103.
[27] *Calendar of State Papers, Spain,* Volume 11, 1553, 6 September 1553.
[28] M.A. Everett-Wood, *Letters of Royal and Illustrious Ladies,* Volume 3, pp. 279-280.
[29] *Calendar of State Papers, Spain,* Volume 11, 9 September 1553.
[30] *Letters and Papers, Foreign and Domestic, Henry VIII,* Volume 13 Part 2, n. 1036.
[31] *Calendar of State Papers, Spain,* Volume 11, 9 September 1553.
[32] Ibid., 8 September 1553.
[33] Alice Hunt & Anna Whitelock (ed.), *Tudor Queenship: The Reigns of Mary and Elizabeth*, p. 65.
[34] *Calendar of State Papers, Spain,* Volume 11, 28 November 1553.
[35] Ibid., 3 October 1553.
[36] *Calendar of State Papers, Venice,* Volume 5, 934.
[37] Antoine de Noailles to Henri II, 30 November 1553.
[38] *Calendar of State Papers, Spain,* Volume 11, 28 November 1553.
[39] Ibid., 29 November 1553.
[40] Ibid., 3 December 1553.
[41] Ibid., 8 December 1553.
[42] Antoine de Noailles to Henri II, 14 December 1553.
[43] *Calendar of State Papers, Spain,* Volume 11, 1553, 8 December 1553.

Chapter 7: "My sister was so incensed against me"

On 10 October 1553, Simon Renard, the imperial ambassador whom Mary liked and trusted, had offered her the hand in marriage of Philip II, King of Spain. Philip was Charles V's son, and Mary had always treated the Holy Roman Emperor as a father figure. Fiercely proud of her Spanish roots, the Queen dreamed of reviving the Anglo-Spanish alliance and breeding a new line of Catholic princes and princesses with Tudor and Hapsburg blood running in their veins. But before she could agree to marry Philip, the Queen decided to put an end to rumours that she would marry Edward Courtenay, Earl of Devonshire. He was boasting that Mary would marry him, but the Queen declared to the delegation of nobles that she "had no liking for Courtenay" in terms of marriage and told her councillors openly that she would not make him her husband.[1] Marriage to her subject was not what Mary had in mind since she was always very sensitive about her status as a royal princess and would accept no one else but a man who equalled her in rank.

In a conversation with Simon Renard, Courtenay said that "he was too unworthy ever to have thought of so exalted an alliance". Contrary to rumours circulating at court, he was also not inclined to marry Lady Elizabeth, with whom his name was so often linked. He told Renard that he would rather marry "some simple girl than Elizabeth, who was a heretic, too proud and of too doubtful lineage on her mother's side".[2] But Courtenay lied. Mary's rejection was a painful blow to the young earl who believed the Queen owed him a favour after his father lost his life on the scaffold for her sake. He was already planning revenge behind Mary's back.

With Courtenay out of the picture, Queen Mary agreed to marry Philip II. It was not an easy decision—ever since the imperial ambassador proposed this match, Mary had barely slept and "continually wept and prayed God to inspire her with an answer to the question of marriage". Pointing at the Holy Sacrament, which stood on the altar before them, Mary told Renard that "she had invoked it as her protector, guide and counselor, and still prayed with all her heart that it would come to her help". "There was no one else in the room except Mrs Clarentius and myself", Renard later reported. They followed the Queen when she knelt before the sacrament, singing the religious hymn

"Veni Creator Spiritus".³ Mary firmly believed that her decision to marry was inspired by God himself. Renard, on the other hand, believed that she accepted Philip "for the good of her people and in the hope of begetting heirs, rather than from any private inclination or amorousness of disposition."⁴

The announcement of the Queen's impending marriage to Philip of Spain was greeted with discontent among her subjects. On 16 November 1553, some twenty members of the Commons appeared before Mary to dissuade her from marrying a foreigner, but she eloquently explained her own stance on the matter. She refused to be forced into marrying anyone else, declaring that "if she were married against her will she would not live three months and she would have no children".⁵ Mary implied that if she married someone she did not like, she would be unable to conceive. The news of Mary's intended Spanish alliance spread through England like wildfire, and by the end of November it was "considered here as settled".⁶

Mary was curious about the man who was to become her husband and asked Renard to show her Philip's portrait. The ambassador sent for an official painting prepared to celebrate the engagement, although a portrait by Titian had "been sent in secret" to Mary.⁷ On 28

November 1553, Renard reported that he showed Philip's portrait to the Queen on the same evening that he received it from Charles V's courier. Mary, Renard duly reported, "saw it as gladly as if it had been his Highness in person".[8]

Spending Christmas season in the countryside, Elizabeth wrote a congratulatory letter to the Queen when Mary sent her official letters informing her of her impending marriage to Philip. In her letter, Elizabeth first apologised for not writing to the Queen sooner, informing her of her poor health: "I have been troubled, since arriving at my house, with such a cold and headache that I have never felt their equal, and especially during the last three weeks I have had no respite because of the pain in my head and in my arms."[9]

Not everyone was as enthusiastic about the Spanish alliance as the Queen. Mary's marriage to a foreigner was what Henry VIII and Edward VI feared the most, and Englishmen were afraid that Spaniards would rule over them. By the end of the year, a conspiracy aimed at thwarting the Spanish match by deposing the Queen and replacing her with Elizabeth and Edward Courtenay was hatched. The leader of the rebellion was Sir Thomas Wyatt from Kent, son of the much-famed poet. The conspirators were backed by the French King Henri II, who hoped that the Anglo-Spanish alliance could be nipped in its bud.

The Queen's first instinct was to summon her sister back to London. On 26 January 1554, she wrote a cordial letter, inviting Elizabeth to Whitehall Palace to make sure she was safe. She addressed her as her "right dear and entirely beloved sister" and explained that "certain evil-disposed persons" spread "lewd and untrue rumours" inciting her "good and loving subjects to an unnatural rebellion against God, us and the tranquillity of our realm". Mary further added:

"We, tendering the surety of your person, which might chance to be in some peril if any sudden tumult should arise where you now be, or about Donnington, whither, as we understand, you are minded shortly to remove, do therefore think expedient you should put yourself in good readiness, with all convenient speed, to make your repair hither to us. Which we pray you fail not to do: Assuring you, that as you may most safely remain here, so shall you be most heartily welcome to us. And of your mind herein we pray you to return answer by this messenger."[10]

Elizabeth expressed horror at the revolt, but she had no desire to join Mary in London. She suspected the Queen was more concerned in securing her royal person than in keeping her safe. Citing her recent illness as a polite excuse, Elizabeth instructed members of her household to inform the Queen's messenger that she could not possibly travel to the capital in her present state.

In reality, Elizabeth had good reason to fear that Mary knew something about her communication with the rebels. In her letter, the Queen referred to Donnington, one of Elizabeth's estates. Only several days earlier, Elizabeth had received a visit from Sir John Croft, one of the rebels. Croft had delivered a message from Thomas Wyatt and urged Elizabeth to move to Donnington Castle. Elizabeth planned to move there, but her illness made it impossible.

The Queen was angry with Elizabeth's refusal to join her and suspected that her sister was feigning illness. At that time, however, Mary had no time to lose since Wyatt and his army were making their way towards London. She would deal with Elizabeth later.

On 1 February 1554, the Queen rode to Guildhall, where she delivered the most memorable speech of her short reign. Addressing her "loving subjects" in her rough, manly voice, she declared that she was wedded to her realm and that although she had no children, she loved her people as mothers loved their offspring. She then explained that her decision to marry was not dictated by her whim, but because "it might please God that I should leave you a successor". "On the word of a Queen", she ensured them that she would never allow the Spaniards to oppress them. With this speech, Mary had again won the hearts of her people, who cried out, "God save Queen Mary and the Prince of Spain!"[11]

Mary's resolve was so strong that she wanted to fight on the field herself, but this was not allowed. She stayed with her women at Whitehall and once again refused to flee. Whereas the Queen proved that she had great courage, her ladies-in-waiting gave vent to their fears. When an armed detachment of gentlemen pensioners stationed themselves under the Queen's suite, "the ladies were very fearful". They were "lamenting, crying and wringing their hands". Fearing defeat, some of the ladies wailed: "Alas, there is some great mischief towards; we shall all be destroyed this night!" While others bewailed: "What a sight is this, to see the Queen's chamber full of armed men; the like was never seen or heard of."[12] In the end, Wyatt and his rebels were defeated on 8 February

1553. Mary believed that God had her in his care. Now she was eager to carry out suitable punishments. Mary's ire turned towards those who sought her ruin. Henry Grey, Duke of Suffolk, recklessly sealed his daughter's fate when he joined the rebels, and now he and his daughter would pay the price. This time there would be no mercy on Mary's part: Jane Grey and Guildford Dudley were to be executed.

Shortly after the arrests of the rebels, the Queen sent a delegation of lords to Ashridge, Lady Elizabeth's residence. Accompanying them were 250 guards. Mary also sent two physicians, Wendy and Owen, who were to report whether Elizabeth was truly ill. Lord William Howard, Sir Edward Hastings and Sir Thomas Cornwallis found Elizabeth "sore sick in her bed, and very feeble and weak of body".[13] Yet, fearing the Queen's ire, they concluded that "the state of her body to be such, that, without danger to her person, we might well proceed to require her, in your Majesty's name, (all excuses set apart), to repair to your Highness, with all convenient speed and diligence". Elizabeth feared that she would not be able to travel "without peril of life" and asked whether she could wait a bit longer to recover her health. She also wrote a letter to Mary, telling her that she was willing to meet with her in London, but she wanted the Queen to give her lodgings "somewhat further from the water than she had at her last being there". Royal physicians agreed that Elizabeth's request was reasonable. Elizabeth was truly ill at the time, suffering from nephritis. She swelled all over and felt sharp pain in her kidneys; this may well have been a psychosomatic reaction to stress. The French ambassador de Noailles heard that "she was so ill... that her life is despaired of". He also heard that she was poisoned "because she is so distended and exhausted that she is a sad sight to see". When Elizabeth set out from Ashridge on the morning of 12 February, she was "very faint and feeble" and almost fainted from exhaustion.[14]

On 13 February 1553, Simon Renard wrote that "yesterday Courtenay, chief of the conspiracy according to Wyatt, was committed to the Tower, and the Lady Elizabeth set out to come hither". She was expected at Whitehall on 14 February "with an escort of 700 or 800 horses, and it is believed that she will soon be sent to the Tower, where Jane of Suffolk was yesterday executed, whilst her husband, Guildford, suffered in public".[15] Renard had no regard for the pair of teenagers whose only crime was that they had ambitious parents.

Tales of Jane Grey's pious but grisly end were already circulating in London. Clad in black, she died as a

Protestant, but her resolve broke when she was blindfolded and could not find the wooden block she was supposed to lay her neck on. "What shall I do? Where is it?" she cried out, terrified. A touched bystander gently guided her to the block, where she laid her head and stretched out her arms. An axe fell on her neck: "And so she ended."[16]

Elizabeth, travelling in slow stages, reached London on 23 February 1553, the day of the Duke of Suffolk's execution. She was horrified to see "gibbets on which hang some of the bravest and most gallant men" of England. She was sick with worry and feared the worst, but she guarded herself against anyone who tried to kill her. "She caused her litter to be uncovered, that she might show herself to the people", Renard wrote with contempt. Clad in white to announce her innocence to the world, Elizabeth wanted everyone to know her whereabouts and give lie to scurrilous rumours spread by Renard that she was swollen because of pregnancy. "Her countenance was pale; her look proud, lofty and superbly disdainful; an expression which she assumed to disguise the mortification she felt", Renard informed Charles V.[17]

When Elizabeth reached Whitehall, the Queen kept her waiting for two weeks, sending only her representatives to attend her sister. Elizabeth brought her own people with her—two gentlemen, six ladies and four pages—but she felt utterly alienated. Her plea to be lodged in more agreeable apartments fell on deaf ears; Mary "caused her to be accommodated in a quarter of her palace from which neither she nor her servants could go out without passing through the guards".[18] Elizabeth's suite was located beneath the apartments belonging to Margaret Douglas, Countess of Lennox. The Queen lavished gifts and honours on the countess, whom she treated as her heiress presumptive. Margaret despised Elizabeth as much as the Queen did and ordered her servants to remove hangings from the room above Elizabeth's bedchamber and use it as a kitchen. Elizabeth, sick and exhausted, could barely sleep hearing the hustle and bustle of "casting down of logs, pots, and vessels". Lady Margaret's malice went further still when she incited Queen Mary to send Elizabeth to the Tower and made various "reports against her".[19]

In the meantime, the Queen was gathering evidence against her sister. It was discovered that one of her servants, William St Loe, had contacted Wyatt on Elizabeth's behalf, but he remained composed in the face of vigorous interrogation and didn't incriminate Elizabeth. Interrogators "travailed with Sir Thomas Wyatt touching the Lady Elizabeth", but he too said nothing damning. On 15 March 1554, Wyatt was tried for "treason and rebellion" and cleared Elizabeth from all suspicion during a speech he addressed to the peers who presided over his trial. He gave lie to rumours that the rebellion's aim was to kill Queen Mary; he rebelled "against the coming of strangers [foreigners] and Spaniards and to abolish them out of this realm". "Touching my Lady Elizabeth's grace", noted a contemporary chronicler, Wyatt "said that indeed he sent her a letter that she should get her as far from the City as she could, the rather for her safety from strangers; and she sent him word again, but not in writing, by Sir William St Loe, that she did thank him much for his goodwill, and she would do as she should see cause".[20] This was an innocent exchange between Elizabeth and Sir Thomas Wyatt, but the Queen firmly believed Elizabeth to be guilty of far more than this. She sent a deputation of nineteen councillors, headed by the Bishop of Winchester, to charge her with conspiracy, but Elizabeth remained calm and "utterly denied" the charge, "affirming that she was altogether guiltless therein". The Queen was adamant that Elizabeth should suffer the consequences and decided to imprison her. On 17 March 1554, William Paulet, Marquis of Winchester, and Henry Radcliffe, Earl of Sussex, came to

Elizabeth's lodgings and informed her that they had an order to conduct her to the Tower. It must have been a strange feeling of déjà vu for Paulet, who, eighteen years earlier, had arrested Elizabeth's mother at Greenwich Palace. Anne Boleyn never emerged from the Tower alive; would Elizabeth?

Elizabeth was devastated and begged Paulet and Radcliffe to allow her to write to the Queen. She gave them to understand that she believed it was not the Queen who wanted to place her in the Tower, but the Bishop of Winchester. The lords agreed and allowed Elizabeth to write to Mary. This was one of the most important letters that she ever wrote because she believed she was going to the Tower to be executed. It is known as the "Tide Letter" because Elizabeth deliberately wrote it slowly so that the low tide that enabled boats to pass safely under the narrow arches of London Bridge would turn, sparing her from the Tower for an extra day. The letter reads:

"If any ever did try this old saying, 'that a king's word was more than another man's oath', I most humbly beseech your majesty to verify it to me, and to remember your last promise and my last demand, that I be not condemned without answer and due proof, which it seems that I now am; for without cause proved, I am by your

Council from you commanded to go to the Tower, a place more wanted for a false traitor than a true subject, which though I know I desire it not, yet in the face of all this realm it appears proved.

I pray to God I may die the shamefullest death that any ever died, if I may mean any such thing; and to this present hour I protest before God (Who shall judge my truth, whatsoever malice shall devise), that I never practiced, counseled, nor consented to anything that might be prejudicial to your person in any way, or dangerous to the state by any means. And therefore I humbly beseech your majesty to let me answer afore yourself, and not suffer me to trust to your councillors, yea, and that afore I go to the Tower, if it be possible; if not, before I be further condemned. Howbeit, I trust assuredly your highness will give me leave to do it afore I go, that thus shamefully I may not be cried out on, as I now shall be; yea, and that without cause.

Let conscience move your highness to pardon this my boldness, which innocence procures me to do, together with hope of your natural kindness, which I trust will not see me cast away without desert, which what it is I would desire no more of God but that you truly knew. Which thing

I think and believe you shall never by report know, unless by yourself you hear. I have heard in my time of many cast away for want of coming to the presence of their prince; and in late days I heard my Lord of Somerset say that if his brother had been suffered to speak with him he had never suffered; but persuasions were made to him so great that he was brought in belief that he could not live safely if the Admiral lived, and that made him give consent to his death. Though these persons are not to be compared to your majesty, yet I pray God the like evil persuasions persuade not one sister against the other, and all for that they have heard false report, and the truth not known.

Therefore, once again, kneeling with humbleness of heart, because I am not suffered to blow the knees of my body, I humbly crave to speak with your highness, which I would not be so bold as to desire if I knew not myself most clear, as I know myself most true. And as for the traitor Wyatt, he might peradventure write me a letter, but on my faith I never received any from him. And as for the copy of the letter sent to the French king, I pray God confound me eternally if ever I sent him word, message, token, or letter, by any means, and to this truth I will stand in till my death.

I humbly crave but only one word of answer from yourself. Your Highness's most faithful subject that hath been from the beginning, and will be to my end, Elizabeth."[21]

Fearing that her enemies might alter the text, adding admission of her guilt, she struck lines across the blank space above her signature. When Mary learned of her sister's letter, she was "much incensed with her Council for this, and told them plainly that they were not travelling on the right path; that they dared not have done such a thing in her father's lifetime, and she wished he were alive again were it but for a month".[22] She decided not to answer to her sister's letter, to Elizabeth's "great discomfort".[23]

Elizabeth was taken to the Tower by barge on the morning of 18 March 1554, Palm Sunday. "If there be no remedy, I must be contented", Elizabeth said when the lords came for her. Passing through the perfectly manicured gardens of Whitehall Palace, she looked up towards the windows of Mary's chambers, hoping to catch a glimpse of her sister, but Mary was nowhere to be seen. Elizabeth complained loudly, perhaps hoping that the Queen would at least hear her. She "marveled much what the nobility of the realm meant, which in that sort would suffer her to be led into captivity".[24]

The Queen sent three of her trusted ladies-in-waiting to act as spies and allowed Elizabeth three of her own women as well. The day Elizabeth was escorted to the Tower was cold and rainy, and when she caught a glimpse of the Traitor's Gate, she made a show of her loyalty to the Queen. Elizabeth "denied to land at those stairs where all traitors and offenders customably used to land". The lords who fetched her were already out of the barge, but Elizabeth stayed inside. Perhaps she underwent a nervous breakdown, like her mother eighteen years earlier, or hoped that the Queen would be informed of her professions of loyalty. One of the lords came back to the barge and asked Elizabeth why she didn't want to disembark; the other said she had no choice and courteously offered his own cloak to shield her from the heavy rainfall. Elizabeth refused the cloak and stepped straight into the rain, protesting: "Here landeth as true a subject, being prisoner, as ever landed at these stairs; and before thee, O God! I speak it, having no other friends but thee alone."[25]

Elizabeth didn't like to see "a great multitude" of servants of the Tower who stared at her and "with one voice desired God to preserve Her Grace". "If it be for my cause, I beseech you they may be dismissed", she told the Lieutenant of the Tower. After this, Elizabeth sat down on a cold stone. "Madam, you were best to come out of the rain; for you sit unwholesomely", the lieutenant told her, fearing that she might catch a cold. Elizabeth replied that this place was better than the Tower's walls. When Elizabeth finally entered the Tower, "the doors were locked and bolted upon her, which did not a little discomfort and dismay Her Grace".[26]

Five days after her incarceration, Elizabeth received a visit from the Bishop of Winchester and other councillors. They "examined her of the talk that was at Ashridge, betwixt her and sir James Croft, concerning her removing from thence to Donnington Castle, requiring her to declare what she meant thereby". Elizabeth pretended she had no recollection of Donnington being her estate; after all, she had many manor houses that she did not occupy. "Indeed", she said after a pause, "I do now remember that I have such a place, but I never lay in it in all my life. And as for any that hath moved me thereunto, I do not remember". Elizabeth didn't break under interrogation, to the intense rage of Mary's councillors.

The Queen wanted an airtight case against her sister, but, to her disappointment, nothing could be proven against Elizabeth. Sir Thomas Wyatt was executed on 11

April 1554. In his final speech, he requested the Queen's pardon and mercy for his wife and children. Contrary to what was rumored in London, he did not accuse Elizabeth. Quite the contrary—he cleared her from all charges, telling the assembled that neither Elizabeth nor Edward Courtenay were "privy of my rising or commotion before I began; as I have declared no less to the Queen's council".[27]

Wyatt's exoneration of Elizabeth bore fruit. "The judges can find no matter for her condemnation", wrote the exasperated Renard, who ceaselessly dripped false accusations against Elizabeth into Mary's ear. "Already she has liberty to walk in the garden of the Tower; and even if they had proof, they would not dare to proceed against her, for the love of the Admiral, her relative, who espouses her quarrel, and has at present all the force of the kingdom in his power". The Admiral mentioned in this letter was William Howard, half uncle of Anne Boleyn. He shared a close bond with Anne and was serving as an ambassador in Scotland when he received the devastating news of the Queen's condemnation and execution in 1536. Shortly after Anne's execution, William married her distant relative and maid of honour, Margaret Gamage. They were embroiled in a court scandal when William's niece, Queen Katherine Howard, was executed for presumed adultery in 1542, but they regained their freedom and goods. William defended London during Wyatt's rebellion and was created Baron Howard of Effingham by Queen Mary. His defence of Elizabeth stemmed from his loyalty to her since she was his relative. Elizabeth would always be grateful to William for espousing her cause and defending her interests when she was powerless.

With no proof against her, it was pointless to keep Elizabeth in the Tower. She was released on 19 May 1554, the eighteenth anniversary of her mother's execution. She was taken by barge to Richmond Palace and then to Woodstock, where she was to spend the next eleven months under house arrest. As she travelled by litter towards Woodstock, Elizabeth could finally feel relief. She would never forget the year 1554, when she came so near to death. "I stood in danger of my life, my sister was so incensed against me", she would later tell her own councillors when they pressed her to name a successor.[28]

NOTES

[1] *Calendar of State Papers, Spain, Volume 11,* 1553, 23 October 1553.
[2] Ibid., 12 October 1553.
[3] Ibid., 31 October 1553.
[4] Ibid., 5 October 1553.
[5] Ibid., 17 November 1553.
[6] Frank A. Mumby, *The Girlhood of Queen Elizabeth*, p. 91.

[7] *Calendar of State Papers, Spain, Volume 11,* 1553, 21 November 1553.
[8] Ibid., 28 November 1553.
[9] Maria Perry, *The Word of a Prince: A Life of Elizabeth I from Contemporary Documents,* p. 60.
[10] Frank A. Mumby, *The Girlhood of Queen Elizabeth,* p. 99.
[11] Sylvia Barbara Soberton, *Great Ladies,* pp. 200-201.
[12] Ibid.
[13] John Foxe, *The Miraculous Preservation of the Lady Elizabeth, now Queen of England,* p. 606
[14] Ibid., p. 607.
[15] *Calendar of State Papers, Spain,* Volume 12, 13 February 1554.
[16] *The Chronicle of Queen Jane and the First Year of Queen Mary,* p. 77.
[17] Frank A. Mumby, *The Girlhood of Queen Elizabeth,* p. 109.
[18] Ibid.
[19] James Anthony Froude, *History of England from the Fall of Wolsey to the Death of Elizabeth,* Volume 7, p. 387.
[20] *The Chronicle of Queen Jane and the First Year of Queen Mary,* pp. 69,70.
[21] http://www.nationalarchives.gov.uk/education/resources/elizabeth-monarchy/the-tide-letter/ Transcribed into modern English by the present author.
[22] Simon Renard to Charles V, 22 March 1554.
[23] John Foxe, *The Miraculous Preservation of the Lady Elizabeth, now Queen of England,* p. 607.
[24] Ibid., p. 608.
[25] Ibid., p. 609.
[26] Ibid., p. 610.
[27] *The Chronicle of Queen Jane and the First Year of Queen Mary,* p. 74.
[28] Clark Hulse, *Elizabeth I: Ruler and Legend,* p. 26.

Chapter 8:
"Your truth"

Elizabeth's imprisonment shortly before the arrival of Mary's bridegroom sent a very clear message to everyone: the Queen treated her sister as a traitor and found her unworthy of taking part in the royal wedding. Mary didn't hide that she hoped to become pregnant soon and deliver the heir who would supplant Elizabeth from the succession altogether.

Mary's bridegroom, Philip of Spain, was born on 21 May 1527 to Charles V, Holy Roman Emperor, and Isabella of Portugal. Before he married Isabella, Charles himself was briefly engaged to Mary, his first cousin, when she was a child. A miniature of Mary as princess showing her with a brooch with the inscription "The Emperor" pinned on her bodice still survives.[1] The Anglo-Imperial alliance of the 1520s didn't last long, but Mary remembered Charles V, whom she had met in 1522 during his visit to England, and revered him as a father figure later in her life.

Philip, eleven years younger than Mary, had been married before. His first wife, Maria Manuela of Portugal, died after giving birth to their only son, Don Carlos, in 1545.

Manuela's death left Philip devastated, and he mourned her loss in seclusion, keeping "myself to myself" and feeling "anguish and regret".[2] Soon after Maria Manuela's death, Philip embarked on an affair with a much older woman, Isabel de Osorio, with whom he had two illegitimate children. Isabel was said to have been very beautiful, and Philip commissioned his father's court painter, Titian, to paint Isabel naked. He took her naked portraits to England and hung them in his private apartments.

Philip landed at Southampton on 20 July 1554 and was conducted to Winchester in slow stages. It "rained violently all day", but nevertheless Philip's arrival generated public interest and people crowded the streets to catch a glimpse of the emperor's son who was about to marry their Queen. Three days later Philip met Mary for the first time. Dressed in a coat richly embroidered with gold, he was conducted to the Queen "by a secret way, where she received him right lovingly and kissed him".[3] An anonymous Spanish observer wrote:

"The Prince kissed her, for such is the English custom, and hand in hand they sat down and remained for a time in pleasant conversation. He then rose and kissed the other ladies present, and his attendants kissed the Queen's hand. She was dressed in black velvet covered with stones and buttons and adorned with brocade in front. Her headdress was after the English fashion."4

The next day Mary and Philip met officially during a splendid reception at Winchester Palace's great hall. The Queen was accompanied by her ladies-in-waiting, "not beautiful but very numerous, all dressed in purple velvet with their sleeves lined with brocade". The royal couple "kissed and walked through two or three rooms, and then stood talking for a long time". In the evening, as Mary and Philip dined together, Gómez Suarez de Figueroa, Charles V's ambassador extraordinaire, "presented to them an instrument by which his Majesty gave to the Prince the kingdom of Naples". In effect, Mary was marrying "not a Prince only but a King".5

On 25 July 1554, St James's Feast, Mary and Philip were married at Winchester Cathedral. Philip was dressed in a robe of cloth of gold richly adorned with precious stones, a gift from Mary, who wore a matching gown blazing with diamonds. The prince was accompanied by "a brave following of grandees and gentlemen of his court, so magnificently attired that neither his Majesty's nor his Highness's court ever saw the like, such was the display of rich garments and chains, each one finer than the last".

When he entered the cathedral, he waited for Mary upon a raised wooden platform. The Queen came in procession with members of her Privy Council. Stephen Gardiner, the Bishop of Winchester, officiated at the wedding.

A rich banquet followed with the tables "admirably served, in perfect order and silence", mused the Spanish observer. After the banquet, "which was very magnificent", Mary and Philip retired to their nuptial chamber. The royal bed was blessed in the Catholic rites, and the couple was left alone. "What happened that night only they know", wrote Don Juan de Figueroa to the emperor, adding that "If they give us a son our joy will be complete".[6] Immediately after the wedding news spread that the marriage was "happily consummated" and the Queen appeared content, although she sequestrated herself on the day following her wedding night, as was the custom in England.

Simon Renard, the imperial ambassador who saw himself as largely responsible for arranging Mary's marriage to Philip, observed that the English people were "by nature suspicious and unfriendly to foreigners".[7] Indeed, the Queen's subjects were so suspicious that they feared Philip would become de facto King and England a satellite of the vast Hapsburg imperium. To prevent that from happening, an Act of Parliament proclaimed Mary as the "sole Queen", who ruled as absolutely as if she were King. Mary the Queen was separated from Mary, wife of Philip. To emphasise Philip's inferiority, she gave him the lodgings previously occupied by Queens consort and herself claimed the King's side of the royal household. These injunctions were aimed at curbing Philip's royal power—he was to be Mary's consort and nothing more.

Philip took it all patiently and tried to ingratiate himself with his new subjects. Mary had instantly fallen in love with this tall and handsome man, but Philip confided to one of his Spanish servants that Mary was "no good from the point of view of fleshly sensuality". He found the thirty-seven-year-old Queen, whom he referred to as his "aunt", plain and unattractive. One of the members of Philip's entourage, Ruy Gómez de Silva, empathised with his royal master when he wrote that "it would take God himself to drink this cup", referring to the sexual relations of the couple, adding that "the best one can say is that the King realises fully that the marriage was made for no fleshly consideration, but in order to cure the disorders of this country and to preserve the Low Countries". Still, Philip did his best to assure Mary that his feelings for her were genuine. "He treats the Queen very kindly", wrote one Spaniard, admiring the fact that Philip did his best to pass over the fact that Mary was not beautiful at all. "He makes her so happy", he continued, "that the other day when they were alone she almost talked love-talk to him, and he replied in the same vein".[8] The Queen was in love and believed Philip was too.

Within months, tensions between the English and the Spaniards were slowly becoming unbearable. The discontented Spaniards were offended at the treatment of Prince Philip:

"We Spaniards move among the English as if they were animals, trying not to notice them; and they do the same to us. They refuse to crown our Prince, though he is their King, for they do not recognise him as such or as in any way their superior, but merely as one who has come to act as governor of the realm and get the Queen with child. When she has had children of him, they say, he may go home to Spain. Would to God it might happen at once! For it would be a good thing for him and I believe he would be very glad; we certainly should all be delighted to get away from these barbarous folk."[9]

The Spaniards, who believed in their superiority over the English, derided the Queen and her ladies-in-waiting. "The Queen is well served, with a household full of officials, great lords and gentlemen, as well as many ladies, most of whom are so far from beautiful as to be downright ugly, though I know not why this should be so, for outside the palace I have seen plenty of beautiful women with lovely faces", one anonymous member of Philip's household wrote spitefully. He proclaimed that the Queen was "not at all beautiful: small, and rather flabby than fat, she is of white complexion and fair, and has no eyebrows". He somewhat derided her piety when he wrote that she was "a perfect saint and dresses badly". He also mocked the clothes worn by Mary's ladies, writing that they were "very badly cut". This description of Mary and her female entourage shaped the perception of the Queen for centuries to come, yet it is clear that it was coloured by hatred towards the xenophobic English.

The Spaniards firmly believed that their fashions were the best in the world and were horrified to discover that the Englishmen and women alike favoured French fashions, France being Spain's ancient enemy. When Philip's favourite sister, Joanna of Portugal, sent Mary a gift of clothes and coifs in the Habsburg fashion, the Queen was delighted. The gift was a subtle insinuation that Mary should assume the Spanish identity and dress in the fashions of her husband's homeland. "I believe that if she dressed in our fashions she would not look so old and flabby", one Spaniard proclaimed. His sentiment was echoed by another member of Philip's entourage, who described Englishwomen in great detail:

"The women are tall and slender, their clothes are good and they dress their hair like Frenchwomen, though if they would only imitate unmarried Spanish ladies in this respect they would look much better. Few of them are beautiful, though some are better than others. There are ladies who stay in the chamber and others who remain outside in the ante-room, dancing or talking with whomever cares to keep them company, and every day is the same as far as this is concerned."[10]

Privately, Prince Philip was horrified at the English and French fashions and made secret arrangements to dress the Queen's ladies-in-waiting in Habsburg style, ordering new gowns for Mary's women. The Queen, however, was careful not to adopt Habsburg fashion. She embraced English style to send a clear message to her subjects: although she was half-Spanish on her mother's side, she was an Englishwoman. This was an important issue since Mary was criticised "that she in all her doings declared most manifestly, that under an English name she bore a Spaniard's heart". She spoke Spanish fluently and embraced the culture of her mother's homeland, but she was also well aware that the English people expected her to be devoted to them and their interests.

In November 1554, Cardinal Reginald Pole, Henry VIII's greatest enemy, returned to England after more than twenty years of self-imposed exile. Like Mary, he believed that God had preserved him from his enemies so that he could be an instrument in God's hands and achieve great things for England. Londoners thronged the banks of the Thames to catch a glimpse of the man who had stood up to Henry VIII and whose relatives were killed for it.

On 24 November, Pole arrived at Whitehall Palace in his barge. Before he even stepped ashore, nobles gathered near the gangplank. "The King was dining in his chamber when he was told that the Cardinal was landing at the bridge where passengers bound for the palace step ashore, and went out to the door leading to the landing place, where the Cardinal was already standing, whom the King welcomed, bonnet in hand, with all signs of joy and courteous hospitality, and placed on his right hand", wrote the imperial ambassador. They entered the palace and went directly to Queen Mary, who, "as soon as she saw the cross made a deep reverence to the King and Cardinal who were walking side by side". The following scene was deeply moving:

"The Cardinal knelt: the Queen made him a reverence, bent down to raise him up in accordance with the custom of the country, and she and the King helped him to his feet with all the kindness to be expected on such an occasion; and there was a goodly concourse of people present."

Mary cried as she beheld the son of her executed governess, the late Countess of Salisbury. She treated him with the utmost respect and reverence and lodged him at Lambeth, the traditional seat of the archbishops of Canterbury. This was a clear sign of Mary's intentions since her Archbishop of Canterbury, Thomas Cranmer, "is in prison, for he is married and a great heretic". On 28 November, Pole came before the Houses of Parliament at Whitehall. He had to explain why he had come to England. He, who had been exiled for the past twenty-three years, was chosen by the pope himself to steer England back to the embrace of Rome. "The Chancellor explained why the Cardinal had come, and requested all present to listen to him, who asked the King and Queen, in Latin, for leave to speak in English, and then pronounced a discourse lasting an hour, remaining seated and delivering his words with perfect self-possession", wrote Renard.[11]

Reginald Pole's speech gives insight into his and Mary's opinion of Henry VIII. Pole had every reason to accuse the Queen's father of turning England into "the slaughterhouse of innocence", for he lost his own family to the executioner's axe. But Mary was Henry's victim as well. For years, she hid her hatred of Henry VIII under the veneer of daughterly obedience, but she never forgave him for forcing her to recognise that her parents' marriage was null and void. Mary saw the religious changes in Henry VIII's England as a by-product of the King's infatuation with Anne Boleyn. She hated Anne and never forgave Henry VIII for repudiating Katharine of Aragon. But, above all, Mary never forgave her father for tearing the country apart and introducing religious changes: "When the light of true religion seemed utterly extinct, the churches being defaced, the altars overthrown, the ministers corrupt; yet in a few, and especially in the breast of the Queen's Excellency, remained the confession of Christ's faith". She also believed that her brother, Edward VI, had been but a puppet in the hands of his governors. This belief was misguided, for Edward VI, despite his youth, had a strong personal faith and was deeply devoted to the Protestant doctrine. In a sermon preached by Stephen Gardiner at St Paul's Cross, Gardiner harshly described the young King: "He was but a shadow." The implication was clear: Mary was the chosen one and only Catholicism was the true religion. "See how miraculously God of his goodness preserved her Highness", Reginald Pole rhapsodised, turning his gaze towards the Queen, who was beaming with joy. "When numbers conspired against her, and armed power was prepared to destroy her, yet she, virgin as she was, helpless, naked, and unarmed, she prevailed, and gained the victory over tyrants".[12] Who these "tyrants" were was clear to the assembled. It was Henry VIII, the greatest tyrant of all, who had disinherited her and banished Catholicism from England. Now Mary, his daughter, would undo what he had done. Pole's mission, he explained, was to bring Catholicism back.

In the autumn of 1554 Mary had it all, or so she believed. Finally, after years of misery and unhappiness, she was Queen of England and had restored Catholicism. She had crushed the recent rebellion and had her despised sister under lock and key. The only thing that Mary now worried about was establishing the royal succession. If only she could become pregnant and give birth to a Catholic prince, with Tudor and Habsburg blood flowing in his veins,

"Your truth"

she could be sure her religious changes would not die with her. In the autumn of 1554, it appeared that Mary's fervent wish of having a child would finally come true. "If the persistent rumour of the Queen's pregnancy is true, as it seems likely to be, there will be no more quarrels or disputes here and the thorny question of the succession will be disposed of", wrote Simon Renard to Charles V.[13]

On 28 November 1554, Mary was sure that she felt her baby moving inside her womb when she spoke to Cardinal Pole. That day, a *Te Deum* was sung in all the churches in thanksgiving for the Queen's pregnancy. It was an official announcement that Queen Mary's child had "quickened"—moved inside her belly. The entire nation waited with bated breath for the outcome of this pregnancy. On 20 December, the Queen gave voice to her joy in a letter to Charles V. Addressing the emperor as her "good father", Mary confirmed that what he had heard from her ambassador was true:

"As for that which I carry in my belly, I declare it to be alive, and with great humility thank God for His great goodness shown to me, praying Him so to guide the fruit of my womb that it may contribute to His glory and honour, and give happiness to the King, my Lord and your son, to your Majesty, who were my second father in the lifetime of my own father, and are therefore doubly my father, and lastly that it may prove a blessing to this realm."[14]

The bit about Charles V being her father was far-fetched, for the emperor had failed spectacularly to aid Mary in 1553 when her throne was usurped by Lady Jane Grey. "In all her miseries, troubles and afflictions, as well as those of the Queen her mother, the Emperor never came to their assistance, nor has he helped her now in her great need with a single man, ship or penny", wrote the French ambassador in 1553. This was a sound judgment from a shrewd observer, but Mary was blinded by affection for the man whom she believed was like a father to her. His ambassadors were always her warmest friends, acting as extensions of his own persona. Now Mary felt that she was a great lady who would give birth to her long-awaited heir, Charles V's grandson.

Thirteen years earlier, when she was at her lowest, Mary confided to one of her intimate servants that she had no illusions that she would ever marry while Henry VIII was alive—something she regretted then but certainly was thankful for now. "It was folly to think that they would marry her out of England, or even in England, as long as her father lived . . . for she would be, while her father lived, only lady Mary, the most unhappy lady in Christendom."[15] A depressed old maid with no prospects of children—this is what she had been reduced to in her father's lifetime. But now she was Queen in her own right, occupying the very rooms her father had lived in, for she had triumphantly claimed the King's side of the royal palaces as her own. She had a crown, was married and with child. What else could she have hoped for except for a "happy hour"—a safe delivery?

Christmas of 1554 was the happiest time of Mary's life. She emphasised her growing belly by leaving her gown unlaced in front, as was customary. She was "adorned with her brocades and jewels" and accompanied by many ladies-in-waiting, who wore "headdresses enriched with gold".[16] She gave little thought to her disgraced sister. Elizabeth, secluded at Woodstock, was not part of Mary's brand new, glittering life. But after the Queen learned she was with child, she decided to release both Elizabeth and Edward Courtenay from house arrest before her confinement. The Queen "took to her chamber" in anticipation of the birth on 20 April 1555. Simon Renard wrote to Charles V:

"The Queen has withdrawn, and no one enters her apartments except the women who serve her and who have the same duties as the court officials. This is an ancient custom in England whenever a princess is about to be confined: to remain in retirement forty days before and forty days after. However, it is believed that she will be delivered before the ninth day of next month. She would have liked to go to Windsor, but as that place is far from London, it was thought preferable that she should stay at Hampton Court. Troops will be at hand in case they are needed."[17]

Elizabeth came to court on 29 April 1555, but she was not welcomed as befitted her rank and station. The Venetian ambassador reported:

"As written by me, the Lady Elizabeth came to the Court very privately, accompanied by three or four of her women, and as many more male servants, but was neither met nor received by any one, and was placed in the apartment of the Duke of Alva, where she lives in retirement, not having been seen by any one save once or twice by their Majesties, by private stairs."[18]

The French ambassador de Noailles reported that four days after her arrival, King Philip visited Elizabeth privately. The Venetian ambassador Giovanni Michieli wrote that Philip's "safety and security would depend more on her than any other person". Philip firmly believed that Elizabeth was a better choice of successor if Mary died in childbirth since others were not agreeable to Hapsburg political interests. Mary Queen of Scots was betrothed to the French dauphin, and her accession would inevitably unite England and France, a frightening scenario for Philip. Philip was already toying with the idea of marrying Elizabeth if Mary died, and Elizabeth showed herself willing to accommodate Philip's wishes, for "she is well acquainted with his proceedings and character".[19] Philip could not help but notice that Elizabeth, in her early twenties, was tall, beautiful and, above all, exceptionally intelligent. She had a sparkling personality, good sense of humour and was politically savvy.

When the Venetian ambassador Giacomo Soranzo saw Elizabeth, he could not hide his admiration. "She is now about twenty-one years old", he noted scrupulously in his lengthy account to the Signory. "Her figure and face are very handsome, and such an air of dignified majesty pervades all her actions that no one can fail to suppose she is a queen", he rhapsodised. Apart from her good looks, Elizabeth was also exceptionally well educated: "She is a good Greek and Latin scholar, and besides her native tongue she speaks Latin, French, Spanish, and Italian most perfectly, and her manners are very modest and affable". Indeed, Elizabeth gave the impression of a pious and godly young woman. During Edward VI's reign, she dressed simply and didn't adorn herself with heavy jewellery, as was custom for highborn ladies. John Aylmer, tutor of the late Lady Jane Grey, later recalled that in seven years after Henry VIII's death, Elizabeth could hardly bring herself to wear or to even look at the jewels and clothes he had left her:

"The King left her rich clothes and jewels; and I know it to be true, that in seven years after her father's death, she never in all that time looked upon that rich attire and precious jewels but once, and that against her will. And that there never came gold or stone upon her head, till her sister forced her to lay off her former soberness, and bear her company in her glittering gayness. And then she so wore it, as everyman might see that her body carried that which her heart misliked. I am sure that her maidenly apparel, which she used in King Edward's time, made the noblemen's daughters and wives to be ashamed to be dressed and painted like peacocks; being more moved with her most virtuous example than with all that ever Paul or Peter wrote touching that matter."[20]

"Your truth"

In his account, Aylmer, a zealous Protestant, set Mary's "glittering gayness" against Elizabeth's "maidenly apparel", condemning Mary for what Elizabeth would also do when she became Queen—practicing the "politics of ostentation". Both Mary and Elizabeth were aware that dress conveyed a political message and recognised "that in order to play the part one must dress the part".[21] Aylmer's description also served the purpose of condemning Mary's fanatic Catholicism and praising Elizabeth's Protestantism (although Elizabeth had renounced her Protestant faith in 1553). Mary, heavily bejewelled and dripping with cloth of gold, represented the Catholic Church with its finery; church vestments were, after all, made of rich fabrics such as velvet, satin and silk, heavily embroidered with gold. Elizabeth, on the other hand, represented Protestant asceticism, pure doctrine without distracting and unnecessary finery. Aylmer's description rings true, for when Elizabeth was summoned to court in 1555, the Queen ordered her to wear the richest garments for her first audience with Philip, knowing that her sister preferred simple clothes and dark colours.

Philip was already planning his departure from England. The only thing that kept him by Mary's side was her pregnancy. Renard, who had left England shortly after

Philip's arrival, wrote a letter to Philip advising him against leaving Mary. "Your Majesty must remember the purpose for which you came to England", he cautioned. He then recounted why Charles V made him marry Mary in the first place, reminding Philip of Mary Stuart's marital alliance with France that had to be counterbalanced by Philip's marriage to Mary. "Your Highness, it is true, might wish that she was more agreeable", Renard wrote somewhat apologetically, referring to Mary's apparent shortcomings in beauty. If not beautiful, Mary was at least "infinitely virtuous" and Philip, "like a magnanimous prince", should "assist her in the management of the kingdom". Besides, it was obvious to Renard that Philip's "departure will be misrepresented, your enemies will speak of it as a flight rather than as a necessary absence". Mary's feelings also had to be taken into consideration for she would "not be pleased to lose you", to say the least. Renard's letter contains a curious sentence:

"Should the Queen's pregnancy prove a mistake, the heretics will place their hopes in Elizabeth: and here you are in a difficulty whatever be done; for if Elizabeth be set aside, the crown will go to the Queen of Scots; if she succeed, she will restore heresy [Protestantism], and naturally attach herself to France."[22]

Was Renard already suspecting that Mary's pregnancy could "prove a mistake"? It was an odd thing to say in February 1555, considering that Mary believed her child was alive and moving. The Queen was expected to give birth by 9 May 1555, but the date came and went, and no baby was born. Physicians were summoned to confer with the Queen, and they reached the verdict that she had miscalculated her due date, and the child was now expected to be born before 6 June 1555. "Everything in this kingdom depends on the Queen's safe deliverance", Renard mused in a letter to Charles V. Yet still no baby was born by 6 June.

While Mary awaited the birth of her child, Elizabeth was kept in isolation. Shortly after her arrival, she received a visit from the Queen's councillors, including Stephen Gardiner, Bishop of Winchester. "My lords, I am glad to see you: for methinks, I have been kept a great while from you desolately, alone", she said and asked them to intercede on her behalf with the Queen. As far as Elizabeth was concerned, she was still Mary's prisoner and wanted to be finally set free.

Gardiner kneeled in front of Elizabeth "and requested that she would submit herself to the Queen's grace". This was a veiled suggestion that Elizabeth should admit to being privy to Wyatt's rebellion, but she would do no such thing. She would rather "lie in prison all the days of her life" than acknowledge that she had offended Mary "in thought, word or deed". Elizabeth knew her rights and was well aware that the Privy Council could not prove her involvement in Wyatt's treason. She would never "confess myself to be an offender, which I never was"; if they had proof, they should present it. If not, she should be set free. The councillors departed, promising Elizabeth to convey her message to the Queen.

The next day Mary sent the same delegation back to Elizabeth. Gardiner kneeled again, declaring that the Queen marvelled that Elizabeth "would so stoutly use herself, not confessing that she had offended: so that it should seem that the Queen's Majesty had wrongfully imprisoned her grace". "Nay", she said proudly, "it may please her to punish me as she thinketh good". "Well", Gardiner replied, "her majesty willeth me to tell you, that you must tell another tale or that you be set at liberty". But Elizabeth would not succumb; she said she would rather rot in prison for "honesty and truth" than to be set at liberty "suspected of Her Majesty". "I will never belie myself", Elizabeth proudly declared. Gardiner kneeled again, informing Elizabeth that she should seek revenge on him and other councillors for "your wrong and long imprisonment". Elizabeth replied that she sought no revenge, but she was pleased at her victory over the Queen's councillors.

Whereas Gardiner and others saw how futile it was to exert further pressure on Elizabeth, the Queen was not about to admit that she was wrong in her suspicions. A week after Gardiner's delegation, Mary summoned Elizabeth to her private quarters at ten o'clock at night. Elizabeth feared for her life and asked her ladies-in-waiting to pray for her. With trembling heart, Elizabeth went from her chambers to the Queen's lodgings, her four ladies in attendance and her male servants bearing torches before them. When Elizabeth reached the doors of Mary's private suite, she was instructed to part with her servants. Then the Queen's chief lady-in-waiting, Susan Clarencius, escorted Elizabeth to Mary's bedchamber.

The sisters hadn't seen each other since December 1553. Much had changed since then; Elizabeth had spent eleven months secluded from the world, and Mary was now expecting a child. When Elizabeth saw Mary, she sank into a deep curtsy "and desired God to preserve Her Majesty". She was her true subject, whatever hostile tongues claimed. But Mary appeared annoyed at Elizabeth's protestations of innocence. "You will not confess your offence, but stand stoutly in your truth", Mary scoffed. Elizabeth was not intimidated. If she were guilty, she would "request neither favour nor pardon at your Majesty's hands", she said bravely. "Well", Mary said as she beheld her sister in the flickering candlelight, "you stiffly still persevere in your truth". Elizabeth would not be cornered: "I humbly beseech your Majesty to have a good opinion of me and to think me to be your true subject, not only from the beginning hitherto, but forever, as long as life lasteth."[23] Mary was not satisfied with Elizabeth's answers, and she dismissed her. According to John Foxe's account, King Philip stood behind the arras, eavesdropping on the conversation between the two sisters.

"The Queen's delivery keeps us all greatly exercised in our minds", wrote Ruy Gómez de Silva in early June 1555.[24] Mary was still confined, Elizabeth secluded and Philip also kept to his private chambers since he was mourning his grandmother, the mad Queen Joanna of Castile, who died on 12 April 1555. In the first weeks of June the clergy began to lead daily processions for the Queen's safe delivery. Mary observed these processions from the small window of her bedchamber each day, "most courteously bowing her head in acknowledgment to all the personages". The Venetian ambassador Michieli saw Mary and wrote that she was "looking very well", but others were not so sure.[25] Antoine de Noailles, the French ambassador, learned from the Queen's midwife and one of her chief ladies that Mary was not pregnant because she had often sat on the floor of her chamber with knees drawn up to her chin, a position no pregnant woman could endure without considerable pain. Midwives and physicians were fearful to tell Mary the truth, and so she continued in her false hope. Simon Renard could not believe it, and on 24 June informed the emperor that Mary's "doctors and ladies have proved to be out in their calculations by about two months, and it now appears that she will not be delivered before eight or ten days from now".[26]

Even the most trusted among the Queen's women, Susan Clarencius, flattered Mary's hopes. An anonymous contemporary writer condemned Susan and other ladies who assured Mary that she was with child. He related "how Mrs Clarencius and divers others, as parasites about her, assured her to be with child, insomuch as the Queen was fully so persuaded herself". Only one lady, Frideswide Strelley, was bold enough to express doubts about the Queen's condition. At some point, when she herself started doubting whether she was with child, Mary sent for

Frideswide and declared: "Ah, Strelley, Strelley, I see they be all flatterers, and none true to me but thou." After this incident, Strelley was more favoured than ever before.[27]

By now, the Queen was under pressure to deliver her child as soon as possible. Mary's delivery was "most earnestly desired by everybody, and principally by the King, who awaits nothing but this result in order to cross the Channel instantly, for, from what I hear, one single hour's delay in this delivery seems to him a thousand years".[28] Philip was expected at Flanders in August and he could not bear to remain in England any longer. He started dissolving his Spanish household and sending his servants abroad, to Mary's utter disappointment.

The Queen's prolonged confinement had taken its toll on her fragile state of mind. She firmly believed that her child would not be safely born if the Protestants who wished her ill were not eradicated from the face of the earth. The first burnings of Mary's reign commenced in early 1555. John Rogers, editor and author of the *Matthew Bible*, burned at the stake on 4 February. John Hooper, Bishop of Gloucester—prominent preacher of Edward VI's reign—followed him to death on 9 February. Incited by Gardiner, the Queen signed more death warrants one after another. In early June, there were eight more burnings "to the displeasure as usual of the population here".[29]

In the privacy of her chambers, Mary prayed fervently for the favourable outcome of her pregnancy. Her prayer book, where the page devoted to intercessions for women with child is said to be stained with tears, survives at the British Library, a testament to Mary's faith and a sad reminder of her unfulfilled hope of becoming a mother. At the end of June 1555, even Mary's friend Cardinal Pole laughingly informed the Venetian ambassador that "I know not whether she be or be not pregnant".[30] "If God is pleased to grant her a child, things will take a turn for the better", Renard wrote to Charles V. "If not, I foresee trouble on so great a scale that the pen can hardly set it down".[31] In July, Mary still asserted she was pregnant, although it had been three months since she entered her confinement chamber. "It is now said that the delivery may be protracted until the end of next month, and perhaps to that of September", wrote the Venetian ambassador. He noticed that "all persons seem to have resigned themselves to bide that time, which will never have been too late or wearisome should it please God to render it in the end such as is desired and hoped for by all good men".[32]

In early August, however, the Queen was forced to admit that there was no child and ordered the entire court to move from Hampton Court to Oatlands Palace. By August, Hampton Court was in "very great need" of general cleansing, but the real reason behind the move was the fact that Mary was no longer with child. Giovanni Michieli wrote:

"The fact is, that the move has been made in order no longer to keep the people of England in suspense about this delivery, by the constant and public processions which were made, and by the Queen's remaining so many days in retirement, seriously to the prejudice of her subjects; as not only did she transact no business, but would scarcely allow herself to be seen by any but the ladies, who, in expectation of this childbirth, especially the gentlewomen and the chief female nobility, had flocked to the court from all parts of the kingdom in such very great number, all living at the cost of her Majesty, that with great difficulty could Hampton Court, although one of the largest palaces that can be seen here or elsewhere, contain them."[33]

With no child to serve, women returned to their homes in the countryside, and Mary could leave Hampton Court without causing a grand scandal, although damage to her reputation had already been done. Malicious rumours spread across the country. Some claimed that "this rumour of the Queen's conception was spread by policy" while others believed she was "deceived by a tympany [distension of the abdomen] or some other like disease". There were also those who believed the Queen was pregnant but had miscarried, and some even thought she was "bewitched".[34] Today historians believe that she had either experienced a phantom pregnancy or suffered from prolactinoma, a tumour on the pituitary gland. Phantom pregnancy, or pseudocyesis, is a condition in which signs of pregnancy such as swelling of the abdomen, cessation of menstruation and even emission of milk are present despite the fact that there is no pregnancy. This condition is most likely to occur in women who desire to have a child or are under pressure to become pregnant. Phantom pregnancy seems the most likely explanation since Mary had suffered "from menstruous retention and suffocation of the matrix" since puberty and had experienced painful and erratic periods for years.[35] When she was fifteen, she was "very ill from what the physicians call hysteria".[36] The word "hysteria" appeared first in *On the Diseases of Women* in the Hippocratic Corpus. It was considered a disease of the womb, called "hystera" in Greek. The ancient philosopher Plato explained:

"What is called the matrix or womb, a living creature within them (women) with a desire for child-bearing, if it be left long unfruitful beyond the due season, is vexed and aggrieved, and wandering throughout the body and blocking the channels of the breath, by forbidding respiration brings the sufferer to extreme distress and causes all manner of disorders."[37]

The "suffocation of the womb" was believed to be caused by the retention of menstrual fluids. Mary could have easily mistaken the lack of menstruation with pregnancy, and a tumour that grew inside her belly certainly contributed to her misguided belief that she was with child.

King Philip, humiliated by Mary's phantom pregnancy, decided not to delay his departure from England any longer. On 26 August 1555, he and Mary travelled by barge to Whitehall Palace, where they ate dinner in public. Then they went to the Tower and from there by barge to Greenwich Palace. On 4 September, "the King took shipping at Dover and so passed over to Calais", where he was welcomed by the Lord Deputy and Mayor of the Staple.[38] Mary was deeply unhappy about Philip's departure, but she decided to accompany him all the way to Dover, "constraining herself the whole way to avoid, in sight of such a crowd, any demonstration unbecoming her gravity". The Venetian ambassador, that shrewd observer of events, noticed that the Queen was "evidently deeply grieved internally", and she hardly contained the tears that welled up in her eyes when the Spanish grandees kissed her hand good-bye. When she returned to her private apartments at Dover Castle, she sat in the window embrasure overlooking the river and observed Philip's embarkation. Mary, "not supposing herself any longer seen or observed by any one . . . gave free vent to her grief by a flood of tears". She didn't leave the window until Philip boarded his ship, "but remained looking after him as long as he was in sight". Seeing Mary, Philip placed himself on the ship's stern and "waved his bonnet from the distance to salute her, demonstrating great affection".[39] In reality, Philip was more than happy to leave Mary. "The King of England arrived yesterday between five and six o'clock, in very good spirits, honouring all the ladies he met, holding his hat in his hand almost all the time", wrote one observer.[40]

When he met with his father, Philip informed Charles V that "there is no hope of fruit from the English marriage". Philip now decided to find a suitable husband for Elizabeth, "who is and will continue to be lawful heir unless the King and Queen have issue". Licentiate Gamiz, ambassador of Ferdinand I at Charles V's court, related:

"Now, the great lords of England who might have aimed at marrying their sons to Elizabeth, with an eye to the crown, have been afraid of what might happen to them and their sons, whom they have hastened to marry off in the country, as for instance the Earl of Arundel and two other great nobles have done, believing that thus they were making their sons' heads safe. Thus there seems to be no one open to suspicion at present, unless there be something extraordinary in the offing, which may indeed be the case, given the importance of the issue. Courtenay, who is here [in Brussels], has no heart for the undertaking, nor does it appear that Elizabeth would accept him, for she has big ideas."

Among the candidates for Elizabeth's hand were Ferdinand, Archduke of Austria, younger son of Ferdinand, King of the Romans; Don Carlos, King Philip's ten-year-old son; and Emmanuel Philibert, Duke of Savoy.[41] Elizabeth was privy to these plans and "said plainly that she will not marry, even were they to give her the King's son, or find any other great prince", infuriating the Queen.[42] After Philip's departure, she played the part of a dutiful sister, attending Catholic Masses by Mary's side. In September, it was reported that "the Queen's Grace and my Lady Elizabeth, and all the court, did fast from flesh" and celebrated the pope's jubilee.[43] Elizabeth's first biographer, William Camden, defended her reputation by writing that Elizabeth:

"... Professed herself for fear of death, a Romish Catholic: yet did not Queen Mary believe her, as remembering that she herself, for fear of death, had by letters written with her own hand to her father, (which I myself have seen) both forever renounced the Bishop of Rome's authority in England, and withal acknowledged her father to be Supreme Head of the Church of England under Christ, and her mother's marriage with King Henry her father to have been incestuous and unlawful."[44]

Whether she believed Elizabeth or not, Mary treated her with more kindness than hitherto. In early September 1555, Antoine de Noailles reported that Elizabeth "is a little more favoured than usual". This, the French ambassador believed, was Philip's doing since he had "a friendly disposition for her" and wrote "several letters to the Queen, his wife, commending the princess to her care".[45] Elizabeth remained at court until 18 October 1555. De Noailles reported:

"Everyone believes that the Queen has purposely sent her away so that she may not assist at the opening of Parliament, and also to deaden the people's affection for her. Everyone in London, however, both great and small, made great demonstrations when the said Lady passed through on the 18th day of this month, making many signs of joy and all other customary salutations, and following her out of the town. For this cause the princess was obliged to order several of her gentlemen and officers to remain behind in order to keep people in check."46

Elizabeth left two days after the burning of the Protestant bishops Hugh Latimer and Nicholas Ridley. According to martyrologist John Foxe, Latimer encouraged Ridley: "Be of good comfort, and play the man, Master Ridley; we shall this day light such a candle, by God's grace, in England, as I trust shall never be put out."47 Shortly after Elizabeth's departure, Mary lost her great supporter and friend, Bishop Stephen Gardiner. He died on 12 November 1555 "to the very great sorrow of the Queen and of all good men".48 Abandoned by Philip and mourning the loss of her Lord Chancellor, Mary slid deeper into depression and instructed Cardinal Pole to inform her husband of her "earnest desire for his presence".49 Yet Philip cared little for Mary's feelings, and soon after he left her, he embarked on a series of love affairs with beautiful but lowborn women. The Spaniards now ridiculed the Queen for not wanting to crown their prince as King of England, saying that "the baker's daughter is better in her gown than Queen Mary without the crown". Mary could only wait and hope that Philip would return to her side. He would eventually come back, but not for Mary. He wanted England's nobility to prove their loyalty to him and fight in his wars. Also, he wanted to make sure that if Mary died without issue, England would still be loyal to the Hapsburgs. To achieve this end, Philip planned to forge a new alliance by marrying Elizabeth to the Duke of Savoy.

NOTES

[1] Queen Mary I, attributed to Lucas Horenbout (or Hornebolte) watercolour on vellum, circa 1525, NPG 6453
https://www.npg.org.uk/collections/search/portrait/mw09583/Queen-Mary-I
[2] Geoffrey Parker, *Imprudent King: A New Life of Philip II*, p.30.
[3] Charles Wriothesley, *Wriothesley's Chronicle*, Volume 2, p. 118.
[4] *Calendar of State Papers, Spain*, Volume 13, n. 11.
[5] Charles Wriothesley, *Wriothesley's Chronicle*, Volume 2, p. 120.
[6] *Calendar of State Papers, Spain*, Volume 13, n. 11.
[7] Ibid., 20 July 1553.
[8] Ibid., n. 30.
[9] Ibid., n. 72.
[10] Ibid., n. 11.
[11] Ibid., n. 118.
[12] Henry Soames, *The History of the Reformation of the Church of England: Reigns of the Queens Mary and Elizabeth*, p. 262.
[13] *Calendar of State Papers, Spain*, Volume 13, n. 76.

[14] Ibid., n. 130.
[15] Letters and Papers, Foreign and Domestic, Henry VIII, Volume 17, n. 371.
[16] *Calendar of State Papers, Spain,* Volume 13, n. 127.
[17] Ibid., n. 178.
[18] *Calendar of State Papers, Venice,* Volume 6, n. 72.
[19] Ibid., n. 67.
[20] Lucy Aikin, *Memoirs of the Court of Elizabeth: Queen of England,* Volume 1, p. 99.
[21] Eric Ives, *The Life and Death of Anne Boleyn,* p. 218.
[22] James A. Froude, *History of England from the Fall of Wolsey to the Defeat of the Spanish Armada,* Volume 6, p. 330.
[23] John Foxe, *The Miraculous Preservation of Lady Elizabeth,* p. 621.
[24] *Calendar of State Papers, Spain, Volume 13,* n. 204.
[25] *Calendar of State Papers, Venice,* Volume 6, n. 124.
[26] *Calendar of State Papers, Spain,* Volume 13, n. 216.
[27] J.M. Stone, *The History of Mary I,* pp. 350-1.
[28] *Calendar of State Papers, Spain, Venice,* Volume 6, n. 116.
[29] Ibid.
[30] Ibid., n. 146.
[31] *Calendar of State Papers, Spain,* Volume 13, n. 216.
[32] *Calendar of State Papers, Venice,* Volume 6, n. 165.
[33] Ibid., n. 174.
[34] Sylvia Barbara Soberton, *Great Ladies,* p. 208.
[35] *Calendar of State Papers, Venice,* Volume 6, 1555-1558, n. 884.
[36] Ibid., n. 664.
[37] James Hillman, *The Myth of Analysis: Three Essays in Archetypal Psychology,* p. 253.
[38] Charles Wriothesley, *Wriothesley's Chronicle,* Volume 2, p. 130.
[39] *Calendar of State Papers, Venice,* Volume 6, 1555-1558, n. 204.
[40] Ibid., n. 244.
[41] Ibid., n. 249.
[42] Giovanni Michiel to the Doge of Venice, 21 April 1556.
[43] *Machyn's Diary,* p. 94.
[44] William Camden, *The History of the Most Renowned and Victorious Princess Elizabeth Late Queen of England,* p. x.
[45] Antoine de Noailles to the Queen Dowager of Scotland, 9 September 1555.
[46] Ibid.
[47] John Foxe, *Actes and Monuments,* p. 304.
[48] *Calendar of State Papers, Venice,* Volume 6, n. 276.

[49] Ibid., n. 275.

Chapter 9:
"Anatomies of Hearts"

In the spring of 1556, two of Queen Mary's councillors, Sir Henry Jerningham and John Norris, showed up at Elizabeth's doorstep at Hatfield at the head of an armed guard. They came to arrest her governess, Kat Ashley; her Italian tutor, Giovanni Battista Castiglione; and three other domestic servants, all of whom had been embroiled in the recent rebellion against the Queen. Elizabeth was speechless and frightened ("this circumstance had distressed and dejected her"), but the evidence against her servants was damning, and she could do nothing to stop their arrests. "I am told that they have already confessed to having known about the conspiracy", wrote the Venetian ambassador Giovanni Michieli, adding that "they may probably not quit the Tower alive". Kat Ashley's chambers at Somerset House, Elizabeth's London residence, were thoroughly searched. Kat owned some "writings and scandalous books against the religion and against the King and Queen which were scattered about some months ago, and published all over the kingdom".[1] Elizabeth's name was closely linked with the conspiracy since her servants were involved. Mary now had an opportunity to get rid of her despised sister once and for all, but she hesitated. Instead of proceeding against Elizabeth, the Queen sent Francesco Piamontese, her trusted courier, to King Philip to inform him about Elizabeth's part in the conspiracy and gain his opinion on the matter.

Elizabeth had every reason to fear that this time she would end up on the scaffold. More and more Protestants were burned for heresy every day, and the Queen, still recovering from the shock caused by her phantom pregnancy, sought every excuse to cut Elizabeth from the succession. The most recent victim of Mary's rage, Thomas Cranmer, Archbishop of Canterbury, had been burned on 21 March 1556. Mary perceived him as the chief architect of the Reformation but also held him personally accountable for her miserable childhood and adolescence. It was Cranmer who opened the floodgates of heresy and who annulled her parents' marriage. Mary made sure to humiliate Cranmer before he died, forcing him to recant his Protestant views. Cranmer recanted publicly four times, but when he realised Mary had no intention of releasing him, he returned to his Protestant views on the day of his execution.

Elizabeth's reaction to Cranmer's death remains unknown, but she had every reason to mourn him. He was her godfather and a great supporter of Anne Boleyn, Elizabeth's mother, because he believed that Anne was instrumental in introducing religious changes in England. "I loved her not a little for the love which I judged her to bear towards God and His Gospel", he wrote after Anne's arrest in 1536.[2] It was Cranmer who had crowned Anne with St Edward's crown and who served as chaplain to Thomas Boleyn, Elizabeth's grandfather, before he became Archbishop of Canterbury. Queen Mary never acknowledged the sanctity of Anne Boleyn's coronation and was eager to burn the man who had elevated her to that dignity.[3]

Elizabeth expected that this time her sister would proceed against her, but when Francesco Piamontese returned from Brussels with instructions from King Philip, Mary was thwarted. Philip wanted no action taken against Elizabeth, whose claim to the throne he supported. Mary, who was blindly obedient to her beloved if absent husband, decided to act according to his wishes and affected to trust Elizabeth. On 8 June 1556, she sent Sir Edward Hastings, her Master of the Horse, and Sir Francis Englefield, one of her councillors, to "console and comfort" Elizabeth on her behalf. They assured Elizabeth that the Queen trusted that she had no knowledge of the treason committed by her servants, and presented her with "a ring worth 400 ducats" from Mary. The Queen's message was bittersweet, however. Elizabeth was informed that her servants had "hitherto deposed and confessed", and Hastings and Englefield assured her that the Queen would show her "good will and disposition, provided she continue to live becomingly, to Her Majesty's liking". The Queen's action took everyone by surprise. "This message is considered most gracious by the whole kingdom", wrote Michieli, who also added that Elizabeth had many supporters who wished her "all ease and honour . . . greatly regretting any trouble she may incur".[4] Privately, Queen Mary still harboured hopes that her unruly sister could be married off and sent abroad to Spain or some other Habsburg dominion.

The Queen placed Sir Thomas Pope, "a rich and grave gentleman", in Elizabeth's household to act as her guardian. Elizabeth "accepted him willingly", although Pope "did his utmost to decline such a charge", knowing that conspiracies stuck to her like a burr. Kat Ashley was replaced by "a widowed gentlewoman", Mary's spy. It may have been said, wrote Michieli, that Elizabeth was kept "in ward and custody, though in such decorous and honourable form as becoming her station".[5]

Pope was right to fear his new post, for in the summer of 1556 another rebel, a pretender impersonating the banished Edward Courtenay, proclaimed himself and his "beloved bedfellow" Elizabeth as King and Queen of England. The conspiracy was obviously crazed, but Elizabeth was furious that her name was linked with yet another rebellion in such a dishonourable way. On 2 August, she penned a letter to the Queen condemning "rebellious hearts and devilish intents" of Englishmen, comparing them to the Devil's "imps". She carefully quoted the Catholic version of the Latin Bible authorised by Mary's church so as to avoid any suspicions that she sided with the Protestants:

"When I revolve in mind (most noble Queen) the old love of Painyms [pagans] to their prince and the reverent fear of the Romans to their Senate, I can but muse for my part, and blush for theirs, to see the rebellious hearts and devilish intents of Christians in names, but Jews indeed toward their anointed King. Which methinks if they had feared God though they could not have loved the State, they should for dread of their own plague have refrained that wickedness which their bounden duty to your Majesty hath not restrained. But when I call to remembrance that the devil *tanquam Leo rugiens circumit querens que devorare potest* [the devil, as a roaring lion, walketh about, seeking whom he may devour], I do the less marvel, though he have gotten such novices into his professed house, as vessels without God's grace, more apt to serve his palace, than might to inhabit English land. I am the bolder to call them his imps, for that Saint Paul saith *seditiosi filii sunt diabolic* [the seditious are the children of the Devil], and since I have so good a buckler, I fear the less to enter into their judgment. Of this I assure your Majesty, though it be my part, above the rest, to bewail such things, though my name had not been in them, yet it vexeth me so much that the devil owes me such a hate, as to put me in any part of his mischievous instigations, whom as I profess him my foe that is all Christians' enemy, so wish I he had some other way invented to spite me, but since it hath pleased God thus to bewray [expose] their malice afore they finish their purpose, I most humbly thank him both that he hath ever thus preserved your Majesty through his aid, much like a lamb from the horns of their Basan bulls, and also stirs up the hearts of your loving subjects to resist them and deliver you to his honour, and their shame. The intelligence of which, proceeding from your Majesty, deserveth more humble thanks than with my pen I can render, which as infinite I will leave to number. And among earthly things I chiefly wish this one, that there were as good surgeons for making anatomies of hearts that might show my thoughts to your Majesty, as there are expert physicians of the bodies, able to express the inward griefs of their maladies to their patients. For then I doubt not, but know well, that whatsoever other should suggest by malice, yet your Majesty should be sure by knowledge, so that the more such misty clouds offuscate the clear light of my truth, the more my tried thoughts should glister to the dimming of their hid malice. But since wishes are vain, and desire oft fails, I must crave that my deeds may supply that my thoughts cannot declare, and they be not misdeemed there, as the facts have been so well tried. And like as I have been your faithful subject from the beginning of your reign, so shall no wicked persons cause me to change to the end of my life. And thus I commit your Majesty to God's tuition, who I beseech long time to preserve, ending with the new remembrance of my old suit, more for that it should not be forgotten, than for that I think it not remembered.

From Hatfield this present Sunday the second day of August, your Majesty's obedient subject and humble sister,

Elizabeth."[6]

Inserting Latin quotes from the Catholic Bible was a wise move on Elizabeth's part. She feared that, having no other weapon against her, Mary could turn to accusing her of heresy. More and more Protestants were being burned in England, making Mary more unpopular. In July 1556, a group of women were burned on the Channel island of Guernsey. One of them, Perotine Massey, was pregnant and gave birth at the stake; her baby died with her. Hearing such stories must have made Elizabeth fearful for her own life.

On 28 November 1556, Elizabeth arrived in London for Christmas festivities "with a handsome retinue" of more than two hundred horsemen clad in her own livery. Giovanni Michieli related that three days later Elizabeth was received by the Queen "very graciously and familiarly". Even Cardinal Pole, who earlier failed to visit Elizabeth, now paid his respects to her. It appeared as if Elizabeth was "in good favour with Her Majesty", as befitted her rank as Mary's heiress. It looked as if the sisters were reconciled, but on 3 December Elizabeth left court in a huff. Michieli, who planned to pay his respects to her, "had not time to pay her my visit".[7]

The reason behind Elizabeth's sudden departure was her rejection of Mary's offer of marriage. The Queen, urged by Philip, informed Elizabeth that it was her husband's wish that she marry Emmanuel Philibert, Duke of Savoy. Elizabeth refused. She would not marry the duke or any other great prince named by her sister. She knew well enough that marriage with a candidate named by Philip would forever tie her to Habsburg interests, and she had no intention of becoming their puppet. Besides, Elizabeth had no intention to marry at all. When she was eight years old, she plainly declared to her childhood friend Robert Dudley that she would never marry. Elizabeth's resolve may have looked like a childish whim then, but time showed that she was serious.

The Queen took Elizabeth's refusal as the ultimate insult. She offered her a great prince, and Elizabeth had the temerity to refuse him. Mary believed that she had offered too much, considering Elizabeth's illegitimacy and the scandalous circumstances of her birth. Mary gave vent to her true feelings and threatened to renew her proposal of declaring Elizabeth illegitimate, depriving her of her right to the crown. She also declared that she considered Mary Queen of Scots as her incontestable heiress, revealing plainly that she planned to go against Henry VIII's last will.

The quarrel between the sisters was serious, and Elizabeth immediately fell ill. She had an attack of jaundice and "green sickness". The "green sickness", or chlorosis, was anemia caused by iron deficiency, especially in adolescent girls, causing a pale, faintly greenish complexion and shortness of breath. Seeing how incandescent with rage Mary was, Elizabeth now believed that her life was in danger and considered escaping from England. When she cooled down, however, Elizabeth realised that if she escaped, she would never have a chance of becoming Queen in the event of Mary's death.

Pressure on Elizabeth to marry was resumed when King Philip returned to England in March 1557. Philip brought two of his kinswomen, the Duchesses of Lorraine and Parma. Margaret, Duchess of Parma, was Philip's half sister. Born in 1522, she was Charles V's illegitimate daughter from his affair with one of his mistresses, Johanna Maria van der Gheynst. Despite the stain of illegitimacy, Margaret was recognised by the emperor and brought up by his imperial kinswomen, Margaret of Austria (aunt) and Mary of Hungary (sister). She received an excellent education under their tutelage and would be appointed as their successor in the office of regent of the Netherlands. In 1536, Margaret married Alessandro "Il Moro" de' Medici,

Duke of Florence. Following his assassination in 1537, she married Ottavio Farnese, Duke of Parma. The marriage was unhappy at first, but then the spouses became affectionate with each other.

Christina, Duchess of Lorraine, was Philip's first cousin. Aged thirty-six, Christina was known for her sharp wit and political acumen. She had been married twice and was now a powerful widow who served as the regent of Lorraine from 1545 to 1552 during the minority of her son. Her first husband, Francesco II Sforza, Duke of Milan, died in 1535, leaving the fifteen-year-old Christina a virgin widow. In 1538, Henry VIII fell in love with her portrait and sought to make her his fourth wife, but Christina famously quipped that she would agree only if she had two heads, referring to the execution of Anne Boleyn, who had been "innocently put to death".[8] In the end, the King married Anne of Cleves, but Christina's full-length portrait by Hans Holbein remained in the royal collection until Henry VIII's death in 1547.

Mary and Philip planned to use the duchesses as escorts so that "they might bring back with them Madame Elizabeth to this side of the sea, to marry her to the Duke of Savoy".[9] Elizabeth was widely opposed to such a marriage, but Philip concocted a scheme to smuggle Elizabeth out of

"Anatomies of hearts"

England against her will. The French ambassador got wind of this wild plan and sent word to Elizabeth via Elisabeth Parr, Marchioness of Northampton. The marchioness was Elizabeth's friend and had connections with the French embassy. She was disillusioned with Mary's reign since the Queen had annulled her marriage to William Parr, Marquis of Northampton, because he married her in 1548 while his adulterous first wife was still alive. After losing her husband, title and home, the marchioness was ready to risk the Queen's wrath and showed up at Elizabeth's doorstep in disguise, telling her all about Philip's plan. Elizabeth was horrified and asked the marchioness to thank the French ambassador and inform him that she would rather die than agree to marry the duke of Savoy and leave England. She would always be grateful to the Marchioness of Northampton.

Mary herself was opposed to Elizabeth's marriage to the Duke of Savoy. She was still outraged by Elizabeth's refusal to marry him and was now adamant that her sister didn't deserve a grand match like this—or any match at all. Philip thought otherwise and urged Mary to swallow her pride and try to mediate with Elizabeth. But Mary would not. A letter written in French in Mary's own hand shortly before Philip's arrival in 1557 reveals her true feelings about Elizabeth. Philip bid Mary to "examine her conscience" whether or not he was in the right about Elizabeth's marriage to the Duke of Savoy. Mary bitterly answered "that which my conscience holds it has held this four and twenty years". This sentence was a testament to Mary's true feelings about Elizabeth. She had hated her half sister for twenty-four years, ever since Elizabeth's birth in 1533. Elizabeth was a living, breathing reminder of the hardships Mary experienced during the turbulent 1530s when their father divorced Katharine of Aragon, married Anne Boleyn and broke with the Catholic Church. The sentence Mary wrote seemed harsh even to her, so she struck it out and wrote to Philip pretending that she didn't understand his argument.

Giovanni Michieli, the most perceptive of ambassadors during the 1550s, observed that whenever Mary saw Elizabeth, she fancied herself "in the presence of the affronts and ignominious treatment to which she was subjected on account of her mother, from whom in great part the divorce from Queen Katherine originated". Twenty-one years after Anne Boleyn's execution, Mary still hated her and transferred that hatred onto Elizabeth, who resembled her late mother in appearance and behaviour.

Elizabeth tried to avoid the subject of her mother, but whenever someone spoke about Anne Boleyn, she would leap to her defence. Michieli observed:

"She is proud and haughty, as although she knows that she was born of such a mother, she nevertheless does not consider herself of inferior degree to the Queen, whom she equals in self-esteem; nor does she believe herself less legitimate than her Majesty, alleging in her own favour that her mother would never cohabit with the King unless by way of marriage, with the authority of the Church, and the intervention of the Primate of England; so that even if deceived, having as a subject acted with good faith, the fact cannot have invalidated her mother's marriage, nor her own birth, she having been born under that same faith; and supposing her to be a bastard, she prides herself on her father and glories in him; everybody saying that she also resembles him more than the Queen does; and he therefore always liked her and had her brought up in the same way as the Queen, and bequeathed to each of them 10,000 scudi per annum, and, what matters more, substituted her in the stead of the Queen as successor to the Crown, should he die without male heirs."

Michieli also wrote that Mary "would gladly have inflicted every sort of punishment" on Elizabeth and was partially justified in this since "it unfortunately appears that never is a conspiracy discovered in which either justly or unjustly she or some of her servants are not mentioned". But Mary could not proceed against Elizabeth since she promised Philip she would treat her with respect. Mary's glory days when she was popular were far behind her, and she feared that if she executed her sister, rebellion would break out, so she was forced to accept that Elizabeth was her heiress.

But, although Mary tried to dissemble, her "evil disposition" towards Elizabeth was obvious. It couldn't be denied, Michieli wrote, "that she displays in many ways the scorn and ill will she bears her". "What disquiets her most of all", Michieli observed, "is to see the eyes and hearts of the nation already fixed on this lady as successor to the Crown". The Queen despaired "to see the illegitimate child of a criminal who was punished as a public strumpet, on the point of inheriting the throne with better fortune than herself, whose descent is rightful, legitimate, and regal".

Great numbers of noblemen flocked to Elizabeth's household, eager to prove their loyalty to her: "There is not a lord or gentleman in the kingdom who has failed, and continues endeavouring, to enter her service himself or to place one of his sons or brothers in it, such being the love and affection borne her." Yet Elizabeth was careful not to enrage the Queen, and "when requested to take servants she always excuses herself on account of the straits and poverty in which she is kept, and by this astute and judicious apology she adroitly incites a tacit compassion for herself and consequently yet greater affection, as it seems strange and vexatious to everybody that being the daughter of a King she should be treated and acknowledged so sparingly".

Michieli believed that Elizabeth would make a great Queen since she was good-looking and intelligent. "She is a young woman whose mind is considered no less excellent than her person, although her face is comely rather than handsome, but she is tall and well formed, with a good skin, although swarthy; she has fine eyes and above all a beautiful hand of which she makes a display and her intellect and understanding are wonderful, as she showed very plainly by her conduct when in danger and under suspicion", he enthused. "As a linguist she excels the Queen, for besides Latin she has no slight knowledge of Greek, and speaks Italian more than the Queen does, taking so much pleasure in it that from vanity she will never speak any other language with Italians".

Elizabeth knew how to gain supporters. She had the unique ability of charming her way out of trouble, although Mary was always suspicious and regarded her sister as a dissembler. "The Queen's hatred is increased by knowing her to be averse to the present religion, she having not only been born in the other, but being versed and educated in it; for although externally she showed, and by living catholically shows, that she has recanted, she is nevertheless supposed to dissemble, and to hold to it more than ever internally".10 Mary vehemently opposed the idea of Elizabeth inheriting the crown in the event of her death without issue, but in this, as in other matters, the Queen was deluding herself.

NOTES

[1] Giovanni Michieli to the Doge of Venice, 2 June 1556.
[2] *Letters and Papers, Henry VIII,* Volume 10, n. 792.
[3] After Anne's coronation, Mary referred to her by her title of Marchioness of Pembroke, which means that she didn't believe that Anne's coronation was valid.
[4] Giovanni Michieli to the Doge of Venice, 9 June 1556.
[5] Giovanni Michieli to the Doge of Venice, 16 June 1556.
[6] Janel Mueller (ed.), *Elizabeth I: Collected Works,* p. 43.
[7] Giovanni Michieli to the Doge of Venice, 5 December 1556.
[8] *Letters and Papers, Henry VIII,* Volume 14 Part 2, n. 400.
[9] *Calendar of State Papers, Venice,* Volume 6, n. 866.

[10] *Calendar of State Papers, Venice,* Volume 6, 1555-1558, n. 884.

Chapter 10:
"She hates the Queen"

The year 1558 started disastrously for Mary. Although Philip failed to convince her to support the prospect of Elizabeth's marriage to the Duke of Savoy, he succeeded in convincing her to join Spain in declaring war against France. When the French King learned of England's declaration of war, he burst into laughter, telling the English ambassador that Mary would have done anything to please her Hapsburg husband. Early in 1558 England lost Calais, its last outpost in France. Calais had been in England's possession since the reign of King Edward III and was wholly English. Its loss was a huge blow to the Englishmen, who hated Philip for embroiling England in his wars and Mary for giving her approval. When she learned of the loss of Calais, Mary said that after her death the word "Calais" would be found etched on her heart. This anecdote illustrates that the Queen was aware of her political failure.

When Philip left England for the second time, Mary believed she was with child again. "They say it is quite certain that she is pregnant, although she tries to keep it a secret", wrote Pedro de Ocaña, a Spanish diplomat who had an audience with the Queen on 25 February 1558.¹ In December 1557, Mary herself confirmed the news when she sent her courier to Philip to inform him that she reckoned herself to be around seven months pregnant. Yet she carefully avoided confirming her condition to her courtiers, although they suspected she was with child. Pedro de Ocaña speculated that Mary would give birth in late February or in early March and insisted he learned it from Susan Clarencius, who was present during the audience. The Venetian ambassador at Philip's court reported:

"The Count de Feria tells me that his going to England is for several causes, the first to congratulate the Queen on the advice given by her these Christmas holidays to his Majesty of her being pregnant, which thing she has chosen to keep secret until now, a period of seven months, in order to be quite sure of the fact, lest the like should happen as last time, when this thing was published all over the world, and then did not prove true, whereas now, having very sure signs of it, she willed to acquaint his Majesty with the circumstance."²

The Queen believed she would give birth in March and summoned Elizabeth to court, as she had three years earlier, to witness her triumph. Elizabeth arrived on 28 February accompanied by a "great company of lords and noblemen and noblewomen" and stayed at Somerset House.[3]

Gómez Suárez de Figueroa y Córdoba, Count de Feria, Philip's ambassador who came to England to keep the King informed about everyday occurrences at Mary's court, suspected that the Queen deluded herself that she was pregnant. "The one thing that matters to her is that your Majesty should come hither", Feria wrote, "and it seems to me she is making herself believe that she is with child, although she does not own up to it".[4]

This time Mary decided to keep her pregnancy a secret and shared the news only with those whom she trusted. For some unknown reason, perhaps when she heard rumours that the Queen was mistaken again, Elizabeth left London on 4 March 1558, accompanied by her large retinue. The next time she would return to London it would be as Queen of England.

On 30 March, Mary still believed she was pregnant, and made her last will. The document was composed in anticipation of the birth of her heir. Childbirth was a risky business, and Mary was forty-two. Her grandmother and two stepmothers perished as a result of childbed fever, and they had been younger than Mary. The Queen, "foreseeing the great danger which by God's ordinance remain to all women in their travail of children", made necessary provisions for the succession. Her crown was to devolve "unto the heirs, issue and fruit of my body, according to the laws of this realm".[5]

In a memorandum composed at the time when Mary believed to have been pregnant, Simon Renard pointed out to Philip that Elizabeth, although an undesirable successor, was a better candidate for Queen than other prospective heirs. He wrote:

"The succession to the throne of England is a matter of such importance that your Majesty will certainly wish to examine the question in all its bearings, especially in view of the uncertainty and danger attending all developments in that country, on the assumption (which God forbid!) that the Queen will die without issue, in which case Elizabeth will be called to the throne in virtue of the will of Henry VIII, confirmed by Parliament in spite of the taint of illegitimacy.

Now, Elizabeth was brought up in the doctrines of the new religion, she was formerly of the French faction, she hates the Queen and has many supporters who are suspect from the point of view of religion. If she succeeds and marries an Englishman, religion will be undermined, everything sacred profaned, Catholics ill-treated, churchmen driven out, those monasteries which have been restored will again suffer, churches will be destroyed, affairs which had taken a favourable turn will once more be compromised. The heretics have no other intentions. Moreover, the ancient amity, good neighbourliness and understanding that have so far been maintained, albeit with difficulty, between England and your Majesty's realms, will not only be impaired but disappear altogether. The French faction will prevail and your Majesty's interests will suffer so much, unless timely measures are taken, that no lasting good can be hoped from this holy marriage, divine rather than human."[6]

Philip agreed with Renard and took it upon himself to convince Mary that she must insist on the Savoy match and appoint Elizabeth as heir heiress. But Mary refused. Determined to overcome the personal prejudice that blinded the Queen, Philip instructed his confessor, Francisco Bernarda de Fresneda, to remain in England and convince Mary to treat Elizabeth as befitted her rank. Yet Fresneda "found the Queen utterly averse to give Lady

Elizabeth any hope of the succession, obstinately maintaining that she was neither her sister nor the daughter of the Queen's father, King Henry, nor would she hear of favouring her, as she was born of an infamous woman, who had so greatly outraged the Queen her mother, and herself".[7] Mary would not allow Anne Boleyn's daughter to take her place on the throne and could not understand how Philip even could ask such a thing of her.

Mary made it her habit to talk to her ladies-in-waiting about her turbulent childhood, recalling her mother's advice and piety, as well as reliving the moments of humiliation she endured when Anne Boleyn was her father's wife. She also talked a lot about Elizabeth. "Queen Mary would never call her sister, nor be persuaded she was her father's daughter", recorded the Queen's maid of honour, Jane Dormer, in her memoir. Jane was one of Mary's favourite servants; she slept in the Queen's bedchamber, read books and religious texts to her, cared for her jewels and personal belongings and was a carver at the Queen's table. "She would say", Jane recalled, that Elizabeth "had the face and countenance of Mark Smeaton, who was a very handsome man".[8] Smeaton was a musician executed as Anne Boleyn's lover in 1536, the only one who confessed to having had sex with her. This was uncharitable on Mary's part, as some observers believed that Elizabeth resembled Henry VIII more than Mary did.

Both sisters, however, shared some physical traits that made them undeniably recognizable as Tudors. Elizabeth's red hair was Henry's, and one observer once remarked that she looked like her grandfather, Henry VII. Mary, on the other hand, was "in face like her father, especially about the mouth".[9]

During the spring of 1558, Mary's health began to deteriorate. "She is somewhat better than she was a few days ago, but she sleeps badly, is weak and suffers from melancholy", wrote the Count de Feria to Philip on 1 May 1558.[10] The Queen was further agitated when an embassy arrived from Gustavus Vasa of Sweden soliciting Elizabeth's hand for his heir, Eric. The Swedish ambassador didn't request an audience with the Queen and went to see Elizabeth before seeking Mary's permission. Yet Elizabeth prudently expressed her wish not to marry, informing the Queen via Sir Thomas Pope that "I so well like this [single] estate, as I persuade myself there is not any kind of life comparable unto it".[11] "Now that the Lady Elizabeth has answered that she does not wish to marry, the Queen has calmed down; but she takes a most passionate interest in the affair", wrote Feria.

"She hates the Queen"

It was difficult for Mary to accept that all eyes were now on Elizabeth as prospective Queen of England. "She now realises that her pregnancy has come to nothing", Feria informed Philip. Mary was also afraid that her husband would further press for Elizabeth's marital alliance with the Duke of Savoy.[12] Depressed over the loss of her supposed second pregnancy, Mary drew consolation from Philip's planned visit to England. When Feria informed her that Philip would not come after all, she took it with surprising calmness. "The Queen has taken patiently your Majesty's decision not to come for the present", he wrote. However, she made necessary arrangements in case Philip changed his mind; a fleet of ships was ready to escort him to England, and lodgings for him were prepared at Dover and other places were Philip would stay on his way towards London.

On 17 May 1558, Mary moved from Greenwich to St James's Palace, visiting Cardinal Pole at Lambeth on her way "in one of the heaviest rain storms ever seen". "She is suffering from her usual ailments", Feria observed in a detailed dispatch.[13] In early June, he reported to Philip that Mary was "worse than usual". The Queen wrote to her husband on a regular basis, and when several days elapsed and Philip received no letters from Mary, he grew worried.

"I am sending the present courier to ask you to inform the Queen that I am well and to give me news of her health", he wrote to Feria. "She has not written to me for some days past, and I cannot help being anxious."[14] At the end of June, it appeared that Mary rallied. "The Queen is better than she has been recently", Feria informed Philip after three weeks of hiatus.[15]

In late August 1558, however, the Queen became feverish and took to her bed at St James's Palace. In a report to Philip, Reginald Pole wrote that "the physicians were and are of the opinion that through this malady she will obtain relief from her habitual indisposition". Pole also wrote that:

"During her malady the Queen did not fail to take the greatest care of herself, following the advice of the physicians; and by continuing to do so it is hoped she will recover, and daily more and more establish her health; a result to which nothing can contribute more than to receive frequent good news of his Majesty."[16]

In October, however, it became clear that Mary was dying. Perhaps the vicious influenza epidemic that swept through England that autumn weakened her already fragile health. It's also possible that the symptoms Mary mistook for pregnancy were the manifestations of the illness that killed her, possibly an ovarian cyst. "Since the Queen's illness reached its climax, she has had some good intervals, and there have been days when she was free of the paroxysms from which she had suffered", Feria informed Philip on 7 November.[17]

As she lay dying in her bedchamber, surrounded by her faithful ladies-in-waiting, the Queen was pressured to name Elizabeth as her successor. Mary's advisors feared that if she failed to name Elizabeth as the next Queen, a civil war would break out. The threat of another War of the Roses, with various claimants bickering over the crown, loomed large over England as the Queen struggled to accept the inevitable.

When it finally dawned on her that her days were numbered, Mary added a codicil to her last will. She now accepted that she was not with child but hoped that she would recover and produce heirs: "Forasmuch as God hath hitherto sent me no fruit nor heir of my body, it is only in his Divine Providence whether I shall have any or not." Mary now had to face the prospect she always dreaded— that she would die childless:

"If it shall please Almighty God to call me to his mercy out of this transitory life without issue and heir of my body lawfully begotten, then I most instantly per viscera misericordiae Dei [by the tender mercy of our God], require my next heir and successor, by the laws and statutes of this realm..."[18]

Still, Mary could not bring herself to name Elizabeth by name, but it was clear to everyone that the Queen meant her sister when she appointed her heir "by the laws and statutes of this realm". Still, that was not enough: it was of utmost importance for Mary to name Elizabeth; there could be no ambiguity about her last will. On 6 November, the Queen received a delegation of her chief councillors in her bedchamber, urging her "to make certain declarations in favour of the Lady Elizabeth concerning the succession". The Queen finally consented. Deep down in her heart, she knew Elizabeth was her sister and a Tudor. Mary herself had ascended to the throne in 1553 via the terms of Henry VIII's last will, overthrowing Lady Jane Grey, who had been appointed heiress by Edward VI. Now there was no other option but to honour Henry VIII's last will again.

Elizabeth was residing at Hatfield when Mary was dying at St James's Palace. She knew perfectly well that her accession was a matter of days, perhaps weeks away, having been informed of the Queen's deteriorating health by her friends at court. But Elizabeth wasn't sure if her sister would name her as heiress, and she began organising support. Just like Mary five years earlier, Elizabeth expected to fight for her crown if need be. For all she knew, Mary could appoint anyone whom she saw fit to wear their father's crown: Mary Queen of Scots, Frances Grey or one of her two daughters, Margaret Douglas or one of her sons; it was all still in the air. Elizabeth soon left Hatfield for Brocket Hall, where she established her operational headquarters. If she could not take over peacefully, she would fight for her royal inheritance. In the end, however, the Queen recognised her as heiress.

On 7 November, Elizabeth was visited by the Comptroller of the Queen's Household and Master of the Rolls; they came to inform her that the Queen had appointed her as her successor but required two things of her: that she would maintain the Catholic religion and that she would pay Mary's debts.[19] Jane Dormer later recalled that Queen Mary sent her to Elizabeth "to tell her who was to succeed her in the kingdom" and give her royal jewellery as confirmation of her last will.[20] Whereas it seems likely that Jane Dormer was appointed to give Elizabeth Mary's jewellery, Jane gave herself too much importance in her memoir. She was not the one who informed Elizabeth that she was to be Queen; this was a matter of state, and Mary sent her councillors to Elizabeth to give her this important news.

On 13 November, Mary's health worsened. There was no hope for her recovery, and "many personages of the kingdom flocked to the house of Milady Elizabeth, the crowd constantly increasing with great frequency".[21] Philip sent his own physician to treat Mary, but it was too late. In a letter to his sister Joanna, Dowager Princess of Portugal, Philip wrote:

"The Queen, my wife, has been ill; and although she has recovered somewhat, her infirmities are such that grave fears must be entertained on her score, as a physician I sent to her with Count Feria writes to me. All these happenings are perplexing to me, and I am obliged to ponder much on the government to be provided for the Low Countries, and also on what I must do in England, in the event either of the Queen's survival or of her death, for these are questions of the greatest importance, on which the welfare of my realms depends. I will say nothing of my own peace and quiet, which matters little in this connexion."[22]

Drifting in and out of consciousness, Mary talked to her maid, Jane Dormer. The Queen knew that Philip's ambassador, the Count de Feria, intended to marry Jane. Mary wanted to attend their wedding, but it was also her great wish to have Philip by her side, so she kept delaying their nuptials, waiting for her husband's arrival. As she lay dying, it occurred to Mary that she was the reason why Mistress Dormer was not married yet. Mary told Jane that "she would have been glad to have seen her marriage effected in her days; but God Almighty would otherwise dispose, and being sick and the King absent, she was not in case to do what she would".[23] In her last moments, the Queen did not think about herself, but about the women who dedicated their lives to her service:

"She comforted those of them that grieved about her; she told them what good dreams she had, seeing many little children like angels play before her, singing pleasing notes, giving her more than earthly comfort; and thus persuaded all, ever to have the holy fear of God before their eyes, which would free them from all evil, and be a curb to all temptation. She asked them to think that whatsoever came to them was by God's permission; and ever to have confidence that He would in mercy turn all to the best."[24]

During her last hours, Mary heard Mass in her bedchamber. Jane Dormer affirmed that the Queen "heard it with so good attention, zeal, and devotion" and retained "the quickness of her senses and memory".[25] Yet the Count de Feria informed Philip that the Queen was "unconscious most of the time since I arrived [9 November]".[26] The Queen received extreme unction on 15 November, and the next day her last will was read out in the presence of her household, although Mary was unconscious at the time. News of Mary's mortal illness spread throughout Europe like wildfire. Michiel Surian, Venetian ambassador at Philip's court, heard that "her malady is evidently incurable, and will end her life sooner or later, according to the increase or decrease of her mental anxieties, which harass her more than the disease, however dangerous it may be."[27] Indeed, Mary had suffered from severe anxiety and depression since she was a teenager. Her fragile mental state was further aggravated by the fact that she knew Elizabeth was to succeed her. But the factor that contributed the most to her demise was Philip's absence, and it was widely reported that she missed him dearly and despaired that he was not by her side during her last days.

The Queen breathed her last on 17 November 1558 at seven o'clock in the morning. She slipped so peacefully away that only her physician noticed that she was dead; others thought she was sleeping. It was reported that Mary "made her passage so tranquilly that had not a physician remarked it on its commencement, all the other persons present would have thought her better, and that she would fain sleep".[28]

At Hatfield, Elizabeth awaited news from court. She was cautious not to take any steps towards her recognition as Queen until she was absolutely sure that Mary was dead. If she proclaimed herself Queen while Mary was still alive, or worse, after the Queen recovered, it could be used against Elizabeth and construed as treason. To avoid such a situation, she secretly employed her trusted servant, Sir Nicholas Throckmorton, to bring her the news of Mary's passing as soon as it occurred. Elizabeth bade him "to hasten to the palace and request one of the ladies of the bedchamber, who was in her confidence, if the Queen were really dead, to send her, as a token, the black enamelled ring which Her Majesty wore night and day".[29]

In her last moments, the Queen was surrounded by faithful ladies-in-waiting who had been part of her household before her accession. Susan Clarencius had served Mary since her teenaged years and was "a woman respected and beloved by the Queen".[30] Others, like Frideswide Strelley, Barbara Hawke, Eleanor Kempe and

Jane Dormer were also among the most trusted women of the Queen's bedchamber. One of them slipped the ring from Mary's dead hand and gave it to Throckmorton.

Before Mary's body was cold, Throckmorton galloped at full speed from St James's Palace to Hatfield. When he arrived, however, he learned that members of the Privy Council had reached Elizabeth before him, and he regretfully recorded in his biographical poem that "my news was stale".[31] According to a legend recorded seventy years later, Mary's councillors approached Elizabeth as she walked in the nearby park. Swathed in fur to ward off the autumn chill, Elizabeth stood beneath an oak tree when the councillors knelt before her, informing her that the Queen, her royal sister, was dead. Overcome by emotion, Elizabeth knelt on the grass, turned her gaze towards heaven and quoted from Psalm 118, verse 23: "This is the Lord's doing and it is marvellous in our eyes." It was an apt quotation, as the previous verse read: "The same stone which the builders refused is become the headstone in the corner." It seemed unbelievable that the daughter of an executed adulteress, proclaimed illegitimate by her father and almost disinherited by her sister, was now Queen. Finally, after five years of living in constant fear of Mary, Elizabeth could breathe a sigh of relief. She was, at last, safe.

NOTES

[1] Sylvia Barbara Soberton, *Great Ladies*, p. 210.
[2] *Calendar of State Papers, Venice*, Volume 6, 1555-1558 n. 1142.
[3] *The Diary of Henry Machyn*, pp. 166-167.
[4] *Calendar of State Papers, Spain*, Volume 13, 1554-1558., n. 413.
[5] David Loades, *Mary Tudor*, p. 302.
[6] *Calendar of State Papers, Spain*, Volume 13, 1554-1558., n. 417.
[7] *Calendar of State Papers, Venice*, Volume 6, 1555-1558 n. 1274.
[8] Henry Clifford, *The Life of Jane Dormer, Duchess of Feria*, p. 80.
[9] *Letters and Papers, Henry VIII*, Volume 16, n. 1253.
[10] *Calendar of State Papers, Spain*, Volume 13, 1554-1558., n. 425.
[11] Frank A. Mumby, *The Girlhood of Queen Elizabeth*, p. 237.
[12] *Calendar of State Papers, Spain*, Volume 13, 1554-1558., n. 425.
[13] Ibid., n. 435.
[14] Ibid., n. 450.
[15] Ibid., n. 451.
[16] *Calendar of State Papers, Venice*, Volume 6, 1555-1558 n. 1264.
[17] *Calendar of State Papers, Spain*, Volume 13, 1554-1558., n. 498.
[18] David Loades, *Mary Tudor*, pp. 381-382.
[19] *Calendar of State Papers, Spain*, Volume 13, 1554-1558., n. 498.
[20] Henry Clifford, *The Life of Jane Dormer, Duchess of Feria*, p. 80.
[21] *Calendar of State Papers, Venice*, Volume 6, 1555-1558 n. 1285.
[22] *Calendar of State Papers, Spain*, Volume 13, 1554-1558., n. 502.
[23] Henry Clifford, *The Life of Jane Dormer, Duchess of Feria*, p. 71.
[24] Ibid., p. 70.
[25] Ibid., p. 71.
[26] *Calendar of State Papers, Spain (Simancas)*, Volume 1, 1558-1567, n.1.
[27] *Calendar of State Papers, Venice*, Volume 6, 1555-1558 n. 1287.
[28] Ibid.
[29] Agnes Strickland, *Lives of the Queens of England: From the Norman Conquest*, Volumes 6-7, p. 103.
[30] Henry Clifford, *The Life of Jane Dormer, Duchess of Feria*, p. 109.
[31] Agnes Strickland, op. cit.

Epilogue:
Elizabeth after Mary

Elizabeth's reaction to Mary's death was one of amazement. Their lives and fates had been intertwined since her birth in 1533. "My lords, the law of nature moves me to sorrow for my sister", she told the councillors who gathered at Hatfield on 17 November 1558. Like Mary before her, Elizabeth saw her accession as God's doing. "I am God's creature, ordained to obey His appointment", she proclaimed. "I will thereto yield, desiring from the bottom of my heart that I may have assistance of His grace to be the minister of His heavenly will in this office now committed to me". Yet she was also aware that her new role was demanding: "the burden that is fallen upon me makes me amazed."[1]

In the days following Mary's death, when the Queen's body was embalmed and laid out in the Privy Chamber at St James's Palace, rumours started circulating at court. The Count de Feria suspected these rumours originated at the highest level and had Elizabeth's tacit approval. He informed Philip that anti-Spanish sentiment still lingered on at court and that Mary's memory was tarnished by the recent political disaster:

"The people are wagging their tongues a good deal about the late Queen having sent great sums of money to your Majesty, and that I have sent 200,000 ducats since I have been here. They say that it is through your Majesty that the country is in such want and that Calais was lost, and also that through your not coming to see the Queen our lady, she died of sorrow."

These rumours perplexed Feria, who decided to keep a low profile "until things settle down and I see who is to take the lead."[2] Feria clearly did not expect kind treatment from the new regime. When he visited Elizabeth on 14 November 1558, he described himself as being received like an emissary "who bears bulls from a dead pope". Elizabeth, whom he described as "a very strange sort of woman", gave him a frosty reception. She was usually composed and rarely let anyone, especially foreign ambassadors, know her true feelings, but she made it clear to Feria that "she was highly indignant about what has been done to her in the Queen's lifetime".

It was undeniable that Mary's treatment of Elizabeth over the past five years had been harsh, but Feria boldly told her that it was Philip who shielded her from Mary's anger and that she should be grateful to him because it was Philip who had defended her right to the throne. But Elizabeth would hear none of it and rebuffed Feria, saying that she owed her position to the love of her people, and not to Philip.

"She is a very vain and clever woman", Feria admired Elizabeth almost in spite of himself.[3] Intelligent, quick-witted and politically savvy, she had a mind of her own and was not prone to manipulation. In a later report to Philip, the count wrote that he thought Elizabeth was well schooled in the ways of Henry VIII's rule. This was a warning as much as a compliment.

Queen Mary was laid to rest on 14 December 1558. In her last will, she requested to be buried with "the virtuous Lady and my most dear and well-beloved mother of happy memory, Queen Katharine". Katharine of Aragon, dead for twenty-two years, had been buried as the Dowager Princess of Wales at Peterborough Cathedral, and Mary willed that her body should be transferred from thence to Westminster Abbey and "laid near the place of my sepulchre". She further requested that her executors should see to it that "honourable tombs or monuments" should be erected "for a decent memory of us".[4] This was not to happen. Elizabeth never moved Katharine of Aragon's remains to Westminster Abbey, a resting place of kings and queens. By transferring Katharine's remains, she would draw attention to Henry VIII's annulment of their marriage and the fact that Mary had passed an act legitimising herself during her first Parliament—something that Elizabeth would never do for herself. Elizabeth let bygones be bygones. She didn't honour Mary's request because it didn't suit her agenda, but she never reburied her own mother with honours either. This only attests to the strength of Elizabeth's character since she was able to separate her private thoughts and feelings from her political persona, whereas Mary allowed her personal feelings to cloud her political judgment.

Although denied burial with her beloved mother, Mary received a lavish and expensive funeral with her favourite cousin, Margaret Douglas, performing the duty of a chief mourner. Her resting place, however, was marked only by the stones from demolished altars, and Elizabeth never erected a monument over Mary's grave, something that attests to how much she disliked her sister.

The late Queen's funeral Mass was given by John White, Bishop of Winchester. He had been Queen Mary's keen admirer and was present at her death, remarking that "if angels were mortal, I would rather liken this her departure to the death of an angel, than of a mortal creature". He delivered an oration, praising Mary's virtues: "She was a King's daughter, she was a King's sister, she was a King's wife. She was a Queen, and by the same title a King also." His speech was based on the verses from Ecclesiastes: "I praised the dead which are already dead more than the living, which are yet alive; for a living dog is better than a dead lion." It was a shocking choice of biblical verse, and its meaning, although cleverly softened by seemingly harmless analogies, was not lost on Elizabeth. The bishop suggested that Mary, although dead, was better than the living Elizabeth. The next day John White was placed under house arrest for "such offences as he committed in his sermon at the funeral of the late Queen".[5] The rivalry between Mary and Elizabeth was not buried with Mary's lifeless body.

Elizabeth was "highly indignant about what has been done to her during the Queen's lifetime", wrote the Count de Feria. In consequence, she did not "favour a single man whom Her Majesty, who is now in heaven, would have received and will take no one into her service who served her sister when she was Lady Mary". She made a show of publicly favouring William Parr, Marquis of Northampton, who had been one of the chief supporters of Lady Jane Grey's claim to the throne in 1553. Mary had pardoned him, but she had annulled his second marriage, contracted during the lifetime of his first wife. Parr's second wife, Elisabeth Brooke, was Elizabeth's favourite friend.

In December 1558, when Elizabeth went in procession from the Tower of London to Somerset House, she made a show of stopping at the window of William Parr's house and talking to him for a long while, "asking him about his health in the most cordial way in the world". Parr, who was ill with quartan fever, could not participate in the procession but was apparently very devoted to the new Queen. The Count de Feria wryly observed that "the only true reason for this was that he had been a great traitor to her sister, and he who was most prominent in this way is now best thought of".[6] In the immediate aftermath of Elizabeth's accession, William Parr was reinstated to his former dignity of Marquis of Northampton, and his marriage to Elisabeth Brooke was proclaimed valid again.

Elizabeth would also show no favour to Mary's devoted ladies-in-waiting. Two of them, Susan Clarencius and Jane Dormer, were Mary's chief confidantes and personal friends. Jane had been tasked to deliver the crown jewels to Elizabeth, but her task only emphasised the tension between her and the new Queen. Elizabeth found that the collection was incomplete and complained of "the deficiencies in the jewels lately in charge of the Lady Jane Countess of Feria, on their delivery into the custody of Lady Knollys, Mrs Norris, and Mrs Blanche Parry". The next entry in state documents corrected this, noting "the overplus of jewels delivered to the Queen by the [same] Lady Jane, Countess of Feria".[7]

In December 1558, shortly after the Queen's funeral, Jane Dormer married Count Feria. The couple had Mary's blessing, but not Elizabeth's. She loathed Mistress Dormer, and Jane had no warm feelings for the new Queen either. The count left London on a diplomatic mission in the spring of 1559, and Jane was to follow him later that summer. In July 1559, seven months pregnant, Jane had her last audience with Elizabeth. The Queen was late, and the Spanish ambassador who replaced Feria loudly complained that she kept a heavily pregnant woman waiting in the summer heat. Elizabeth was later angry with the ambassador, but she had a "very much familiar and loving talk" with Jane. By the time of her departure, Jane had a large household of her own, with six ladies who tended to her every need. Among the women who left for Spain in her entourage were Jane's beloved grandmother and Susan Clarencius, who obtained no licence from Elizabeth. Susan and Jane had developed a strong friendship, and Jane apparently felt responsible for the late Queen's favourite lady, who had no immediate family. In the years following Mary's death, Jane would establish her own semi-regal court at Zafra, north of Seville, and uphold the "blessed memory" of her late royal mistress.[8]

Snow was falling over London on 14 January 1559, the eve of Elizabeth's coronation. The weather had been miserable and cold for days, with rain and snow turning to slushy mud on the streets. Yet despite the weather conditions, Elizabeth's coronation was a splendid affair with a remarkable turnout. The Venetian ambassador Il Shifanoya recorded with awe that the courtiers who gathered to accompany their new Queen "so sparkled with jewels and gold collars that they cleared the air".[9]

Elizabeth was only the second Queen regnant, and she wore Mary's coronation gown. But whereas Mary's dress was loose, Elizabeth had it adapted to show off her slender waistline. Mary's coronation robe was not the only gown preserved (and perhaps worn) by Elizabeth. In 1600, Mary's clothes were listed in an inventory under "Gownes late Queene Maries".[10] By wearing Mary's coronation clothes, Elizabeth emphasised her hereditary claim to the throne.

Mary hated Elizabeth because she was the daughter of Anne Boleyn, and Elizabeth rarely spoke about her executed mother in public to avoid clashing with her sister. However, there was no point in pretending that Anne never existed or in trying to supress her memory. Several stages with allegorical tableaux vivants, where actors re-enacted highly symbolic scenes, were erected along the Queen's entry route into London. One of these tableaux represented Elizabeth's parents, Henry VIII and Anne Boleyn, and her grandparents, Henry VII and Elizabeth of York. They were placed on three floors inside a "very lofty" triumphal arch:

"In the first [floor] was King Henry the Seventh, of the House of Lancaster, with a large white rose in front of him, and his wife, the Queen Elizabeth, of the House of York, with another large red rose in front of her, both in royal robes. On the second floor above there were seated King Henry VIII with a white and red rose in front of him, with the pomegranate between them, and Queen Anne Boleyn, mother of the present Queen, with a white eagle [falcon, Anne's heraldic badge] and a gold crown on its head and a gilt sceptre in its right talon, the other resting on a hillock;

and surrounded in front of her by small branches of little roses, the coat of arms and device of the said Queen."[11]

On the third floor, there was a figure representing Elizabeth herself. In this clever way, Elizabeth did her duty towards her executed mother by restoring her to the place of honour next to her father and tacitly avoided any references to Anne Boleyn's scandalous if unjust death by centring everyone's attention upon her revered grandmother and namesake, Elizabeth of York. This display clearly showed that Elizabeth and her advisors knew how to use propaganda for their own benefit. At the same time, the appearance of the solitary figure of the new Queen graphically conveyed the need for Elizabeth to marry as soon as possible and produce an heir to the throne.

Early in her reign Elizabeth said that she would never rule as her sister did, but she keenly adapted symbolism that Mary had applied to herself. It was Mary who first emphasised that she was a virgin queen. She also said that she was married to her kingdom and that she loved her subjects as a mother loves her brood of children. Mary's speech addressed to her subjects in February 1554, during Wyatt's rebellion, was an example of brilliant rhetoric, one that appealed to Elizabeth:

"What I am, loving subjects, ye right well know—your Queen, to whom at my coronation ye promised allegiance and obedience! I was then wedded to the realm, and to the laws of the same, the spousal ring whereof I wear here on my finger, and it never has and never shall be left off . . . And this I say on the word of a prince. I cannot tell how naturally a mother loveth her children, for I never had any; but if subjects may be loved as a mother doth her child, then assure yourselves that I, your sovereign lady and Queen, do as earnestly love and favour you."[12]

Elizabeth borrowed heavily from Mary's speech and fashioned herself as the Virgin Queen espoused to England and the mother of her subjects. In Elizabeth's case, this symbolism was more potent since she never married and had no children. Like Mary, Elizabeth also often spoke of her coronation ring, declaring in 1561: "I am married already to the realm of England when I was crowned with this ring, which I bear continually in token thereof."[13] In fact, Elizabeth invoked this symbolism so often that when, shortly before her death, her coronation ring had to be sawn off because it was "so grown into the flesh, that it could not be drawn off", it was read by her courtiers as "a sad presage, as if it portended that the marriage with her kingdom, contracted by the ring, would be dissolved".[14]

Mary's motto, *Veritas Temporis Filia* (truth is the daughter of time) was true after her death: Today, nobody remembers her as virgin queen who was the mother of her nation and married to England (chiefly because she married a Spaniard). Only time remembers that she invented those phrases and thus unwittingly helped to construct her sister's iconic image.

Mary understood the power of symbolism, but she never further explored it to strengthen her image. Mary's most eminent biographer, the late professor David Loades, observed that:

"The beautiful likenesses of Mary by Hans Eworth and Antonio Moro are honest representations, innocent alike of flattery and political purpose; while the Warwick and Ditchley portraits of Elizabeth are icons, artificial and unnatural, but pregnant with symbolism which all educated contemporaries would have understood, and most would have applauded."[15]

Mary's portraits show her as she was in real life, whereas Elizabeth fashioned her image as that of a demi-goddess, with her true likeness carefully concealed behind what one historian called "the mask of youth".[16] Painters and miniaturists were forbidden to show the real likeness of the Queen, depicting her instead as the iconic, changeless and radiant Virgin Queen. Elizabeth hated posing for portraits, and "the natural representation of Her Majesty" was forbidden from being painted directly from life. Instead, one officially approved face pattern was produced and inserted into all subsequent portraits.[17] The result is that Mary's portraits show a woman marked by sorrow and aged prematurely. She was said to have possessed "wonderful grandeur and dignity" but this is hardly noticeable in her portraiture.[18] Looking upon us from her portraits, Elizabeth exudes confidence and appears forever young and majestic.

During her first Parliament, Elizabeth was urged to take a husband and settle the succession on her own heirs. Unlike Mary, Elizabeth had no younger sister to fall back on if she died without producing children. She had several cousins on her father's side who were her possible heirs, but she was reluctant to name any of them as her heir. Henry VIII's last will, enshrined in parliamentary statutes, was still valid when it came to the succession in England. If his three children—Edward VI, Mary and Elizabeth—were to die childless, the crown was to devolve on the heirs of his younger sister, Mary, the French Queen. The late King had bypassed the heirs of his elder sister, Margaret, Dowager

Queen of Scotland, with whom he was never on good terms. This went against the hereditary laws of succession. Following the King's death, there were two camps—the Catholics favoured the Scottish branch of disinherited Stuarts, whereas the Protestants declared in favour of the line descending from Mary, the French Queen, and her husband, Charles Brandon, Duke of Suffolk. Elizabeth always preferred the Scottish line.

In the early days of her reign, representatives of Europe's royal dynasties were already clamouring for Elizabeth's hand in marriage. Mary's widower, Philip, seriously considered marrying Elizabeth to keep England within his power. Mary's death was one in a series of devastating blows that he received that autumn; Philip's father, Charles V, and his two aunts, Eleanor, Queen consort of Portugal and France, and Maria, Dowager Queen of Hungary and regent of the Netherlands, all died within months of each other. "It seems to me that everything is being taken from me at once", he wrote to his beloved sister and confidante Joanna, Dowager Duchess of Portugal. In the same letter, he informed Joanna of Mary's illness and of her death. "May God have received her in His glory!" he wrote, adding, "I felt a reasonable regret for her death". Philip had been condemned by historians for his frosty reaction to

Mary's passing, yet his letter reveals more than meets the eye. The next sentence reads: "I shall miss her, even on this account." Several paragraphs earlier, when describing Mary's illness and the deaths of his father and aunts, he wrote, "All these happenings are perplexing to me . . . I will say nothing of my own peace and quiet, which matters little in this connexion".[19]

In the aftermath of these deaths, Philip secluded himself away in the monastery at Groenendael. "His Majesty is so depressed by the death of his father and others, which so afflict him that he does not want to see anyone for a while", observed his confessor.[20] Philip was far from a passive observer of Mary's demise; he had dispatched his Portuguese physician to cure her and obliged him to send detailed reports of the progress of Mary's illness (these reports are sadly lost). It's likely that his chief concern was losing his influence in England, but he couldn't deny that Mary loved him and treated him kindly. He, on the other hand, never reciprocated her feelings, although he respected Mary on a personal and political level. She was his "dearest and well-beloved aunt", and he probably thought about her in such terms. It was a romantic love for Mary and a purely political alliance for Philip.

It has been suggested that Philip fell in love with Elizabeth when he met her for the first time in 1555. The Count de Feria told Philip: "We must tell her that one of the reasons the Queen, now in heaven, disliked her was her fear that if she died your Majesty would marry her (Elizabeth)." In the early days of Elizabeth's reign, Philip took on the role of Elizabeth's mentor, a role that Elizabeth resented. Yet she engaged in political exchange, leading Philip into believing that she might marry him. She showed the Count of Feria great respect, inviting him to court and talking to him about politics ("she is in the habit of talking to me"), although she often slipped irony in their frequent conversations. Philip considered his marriage to Elizabeth in political terms and entertained some doubts as to Elizabeth's fertility—after all, Philip had only one legitimate son and was afraid that Elizabeth suffered from similar ailments as her sister—but Feria assured him that "she is more likely to have children on account of her age and temperament, in both of which respects she is much better than the Queen now in heaven, although in every other she compares most unfavourably with her".[21]

Yet Philip considered his marriage to Elizabeth as a great sacrifice on his part since she was a "heretic"; he would marry her only if she converted to Catholicism, but

Elizabeth returned to Protestantism as soon as she became Queen. Elizabeth put a stop to Philip's plans of marrying her in March 1559. She explained that to marry Philip, her sister's widower, would be to place herself in the forbidden degrees of affinity. It was the same situation her father was in when he married his brother's widow, Katharine of Aragon. Since Henry VIII's "scruples of conscience" (or, more precisely, his infatuation with Anne Boleyn) led him to question the validity of such a marriage, Elizabeth could not marry Philip because it would mean that Henry VIII's marriage to Katharine of Aragon was valid.

Judging from the eloquent speech she gave during her first Parliament in February 1559, Elizabeth intended never to marry: "And in the end this shall be for me sufficient, that a marble stone shall declare that a Queen, having reigned such a time, lived and died a virgin." No one took her resolve seriously, however, and it was not until the 1580s that Elizabeth successfully established herself as England's iconic Virgin Queen. In the same speech in 1559, Elizabeth firmly rebuffed her councillors' efforts to name her successor in the event of her death without issue. Recalling her own experience during Mary's reign, Elizabeth refused to name such a person for fear that rebellions would invoke his or her name. "I stood in danger of my life, my sister was so incensed against me", she said with bitterness, adding that she would never name a successor during her lifetime.[22]

When she fell ill of smallpox in October 1562 and brushed with death, Elizabeth's councillors petitioned her again concerning "my marriage and my successor". In April 1563, Elizabeth replied with a formal statement, invoking memories from Mary's time as Queen:

"Princes cannot like their own children, those that should succeed them... so long as I live, I shall be Queen of England; when I am dead, they shall succeed me that has most right... I know the inconstancy of the people of England, how they ever mislike the present government and have their eyes fixed upon that person that is next to succeed... I have good experience of myself in my sister's time how desirous men were that I should be in [her] place, and earnest to set me up [on the throne]."[23]

Why Elizabeth chose never to marry remains one of her life's most mysterious aspects. She lived in a patriarchal society where women's only aspiration, other than carving out successful careers as ladies-in-waiting, was to marry well and produce a large brood of children to carry their legacy into the next generation. Only Elizabeth knew why she chose a single life. She certainly didn't like the idea of a woman becoming her husband's property and was loath to share her throne with a husband. There may have been other reasons as well. Elizabeth once declared that "for her part she hated the idea of marriage every day more, for reasons which she would not divulge to a twin soul, if she had one, much less to a living creature".[24]

Foreign ambassadors often wrote about the Queen's intimate health, repeating rumours that "this woman is unhealthy, and it is believed certain that she will not have children".[25] Like Mary, Elizabeth suffered from erratic periods caused by hormonal imbalance. William Camden, the first biographer of Queen Elizabeth, who had access to many original documents, recorded the words of the Queen's private physician, Dr Robert Huicke, who believed Elizabeth would never marry because of her "womanish infirmity".[26] Elizabeth often experienced violent stomach pains and bouts of weeping and rage. This evidence, coupled with the knowledge of her irregular menstruations, led some medical historians to form a convincing theory that she suffered from hormonal imbalance.[27]

The Tudors had no knowledge of hormones, but they connected the mental health of women with irregular menstruations. Elizabeth hardly ever had "purgation proper to all women", as menstruation was described by one foreign ambassador, and in 1572 it was reported that she was "troubled with a spice or show of Mother". The words "mother" and "matrix" described the womb or uterus and were understood to mean bouts of hysteria, which in Elizabeth's case lasted "not above a quarter of an hour".[28] These "fits" were probably caused by cramps during painful menstruations. It is thus reasonable to assume that Elizabeth suffered from dysmenorrhea—painful periods. Ambassadors and the Queen's correspondents often referred to her "wonted pangs", meaning uterine cramps.[29] Additionally, she "was subject to a failure [palpitation] of the heart which returned every month", a condition today closely associated with premenstrual dysphoric disorder (PMDD).[30]

In 1603, Edward Jorden published his *Briefe Discourse of a Disease Called the Suffocation of the Mother*, treating about hysteria. In keeping with the Hippocratic belief, Jorden argued that virgins were most prone to hysteria because they were deprived of sexual intercourse. The lack of sexual activity, Jorden argued, created "a congestion of humours" and corruption around the womb. Like ancient doctors before him, Jorden believed the womb was a living organism that moved around the body pressuring vital organs and causing symptoms such as "frenzies, convulsions, hiccups, laughing, singing, weeping and crying".[31]

Elizabeth experienced many outbursts of uncontrollable rage. In 1569, for instance, she was so angry at her kinsman the Duke of Norfolk that she "fainted, and they ran for vinegar and other remedies to revive her".[32] Vigorous sexual intercourse was believed to cure women from hysteria. William Cecil, the Queen's closest adviser, argued that marriage could protect the Queen from illness that usually afflicted women who abstained from sex. He said that by eschewing matrimony, "her Majesty's own person shall daily be subject to such dolours and infirmities as all physicians do usually impute to womankind for lack of marriage".[33] Considering that he said that in 1579 when Elizabeth was forty-six, it is highly likely that he based his opinion on close observation of the Queen's intimate health.

Hormonal imbalance and the lack of proper menstruation are not the only health problems Elizabeth had in common with Mary. Just like her sister, Elizabeth suffered from depression. As early as 1564 she confessed to the Scottish ambassador that she played on the virginals to shun melancholy. Melancholia was not a new term in the Tudor period; Hippocrates had characterised it as a form of prolonged depression while Galen enhanced its definition by adding that it was followed by digestive disturbances.[34] Her depression became more severe as she grew older.

To the chagrin of her advisors, Elizabeth never named her successor. Those who came too close to her throne were immediately dealt with in the harshest possible terms. Katherine Grey, younger sister of the executed Lady Jane, was Elizabeth's direct heiress under the terms of Henry VIII's last will. When she secretly married Edward Seymour, Earl of Hertford, she was imprisoned for life and died in captivity in 1567. Her sons, Edward, Lord Beauchamp, and Thomas, were considered Elizabeth's male heirs, but the Queen proclaimed them illegitimate and never accepted them as her successors.

Elizabeth favoured the claim of Mary Queen of Scots, a descendant of Henry VIII's elder sister, Margaret, Dowager Queen of Scots. But when Mary made a series of disastrous political decisions and ended up in England after her spectacular escape from the disgruntled Scottish lords who forced her to abdicate in favour of her son, she too tasted Elizabeth's displeasure. She was executed in 1587 after spending nineteen years at various properties in England under house arrest. By executing Mary Queen of

Scots, who was manoeuvred into supporting a plot to dethrone Elizabeth after years of futile pleas for release, Elizabeth did what her sister could never do—she executed her successor because she was afraid of her popularity. It was an ironic twist of fate that Elizabeth's heir was the son of Mary Queen of Scots, James VI of Scotland (and James I of England). By thwarting her father's last will, Elizabeth did what Henry VIII always feared and proclaimed the grandson of that "beggarly and stupid King of Scots" as her heir.[35]

When she became Queen, Elizabeth was determined to paint Mary and her reign in the darkest possible colours. The day of Mary's death, 17 November, was to be known as Elizabeth's "Accession Day" and celebrated each year with great pomp and show. Mary's life and reign were harshly criticised by the new Queen's regime. Elizabeth's accession was said to have delivered England from "the danger of war and oppression, restoring peace and true religion [Protestantism], with liberty both of bodies and minds".[36] The implication was clear: Mary was the "bad" Queen while Elizabeth was the "good Queen Bess".

This view was further strengthened by imagery. In 1572, the famous portrait of Henry VIII and his family was used as a pattern for a painting entitled *An Allegory of the*

Succession of Henry VIII. The painting shows Henry VIII enthroned in the company of his three successors. Edward VI kneels in adoration at the King's feet to receive the sword of justice from his father. Beside him, Elizabeth enters the picture, accompanied by Peace and Plenty; she is thus hailed as a bringer of peace and prosperity to the realm. On the other side stand Mary and Philip, accompanied by Mars, the ancient god of war. The painting was intended to be circulated internationally; Elizabeth sent it as gift to her ambassador in France, Sir Francis Walsingham.[37]

Thanks to the martyrologist John Foxe and his famous *Actes and Monuments*, a voluminous work that charted the burning campaign of Protestants throughout the course of Mary's five-year reign, Elizabeth's sister would be forever remembered by posterity as Bloody Mary. She was also known among Protestant circles as "that most ungodly Jezebel of England".[38] Elizabeth saw how Mary's stubborn determination to re-establish Catholicism had created the religious persecution of Protestants, and she adopted a political idea known as *Cuius regio eius religio* (whoever rules, his is the religion). She famously declared that she did not wish to "make windows into men's souls", which meant that she was reluctant to molest the consciences of her subjects.

In April 1559, the Acts of Supremacy and Uniformity were passed in Parliament, confirming Protestantism as the official form of worship in Elizabethan England. Despite this, in the beginning of her reign Elizabeth was prepared to tolerate Catholics. But as her reign progressed, her resolve to treat them mercifully faded, especially after Pope Pius V excommunicated her and released her subjects from any allegiance to her, thereby sanctioning any attempt on Elizabeth's life. Historian Nicola Tallis observed that: "Although Elizabeth never burned any Catholics, she did hang, draw and quarter more than two hundred, thereby bringing her close to level with Mary; many were also imprisoned."[39]

In the early seventeenth century, Jane Dormer, now Duchess of Feria, dictated her memoir to her English secretary, Henry Clifford. By that time, Queen Elizabeth was dead after ruling England successfully for forty-five years. Jane wasn't convinced by Elizabeth's image of a virgin Queen and published a series of denigrating stories about her reputation. In Jane's view, Elizabeth was "proud and disdainful". She cited evidence of one of Elizabeth's servants, who related to her Elizabeth's "scornful behaviour, which much blemished the handsomeness and beauty of her person". It was Jane who suggested that a young noblewoman who in 1548 had secretly given birth to her illegitimate child was actually Elizabeth and the child was Thomas Seymour's. She related how a midwife had secretly been called to attend the birth and how the baby had been "miserably destroyed, but could not be discovered whose it was". Jane's story had an element of truth in it since during the time of Thomas Seymour's downfall rumours circulated that Elizabeth was expecting his child, and there was also a report in London that a young noblewoman gave birth to baby who was murdered immediately after its birth. However, at the time Elizabeth vehemently denied that she was pregnant by Seymour (What else could she do?) and offered to appear at court to show off her slim figure. Jane didn't directly say that the noblewoman in question was Elizabeth, but she strongly implied she was since "there was a muttering of the Admiral and this lady, who was then between fifteen and sixteen years of age". "If it were so, it was the judgment of God upon the Admiral", Jane recorded self-righteously, "and upon her, to make her ever after incapable of children".[40] It has been recently suggested that the woman who secretly gave birth to her lover's child may have been none other than Anne Hungerford, Jane Dormer's beloved sister.[41]

There is no evidence that Elizabeth had children, although rumours of illicit pregnancies and a host of lovers followed in her wake because she was an unmarried, powerful woman. Early in her reign Elizabeth gave rise to such rumours because she favoured her childhood sweetheart, Robert Dudley, who served as her Master of the Horse. In April 1559, the Count de Feria remarked: "During the last few days Lord Robert has come so much into favour that he does whatever he likes with affairs and it is even said that her Majesty visits him in his chamber day and night".[42] The scandal reached vast proportions, not only because Elizabeth invited gossip by spending private hours with Dudley in her chambers but also because Robert was a married man.

Son of her sister's sworn enemy, Robert was said to have been the Queen's lover. When Elizabeth complained to the Spanish ambassador about slanderous rumours touching their relationship, she marvelled how anyone could entertain any doubts of her moral purity since "my life is in the open and I have so many witnesses that I cannot understand how so bad a judgment can have formed of me".[43]

Robert Dudley, whom Elizabeth rewarded with the earldom of Leicester, came very close to marrying her. Yet his reputation was much tarnished when his wife was found dead at the bottom of a staircase. Malicious tongues affirmed that Amy Dudley was killed to enable Robert to marry the Queen. The scandal that erupted sent shockwaves across Europe, and Elizabeth never married Robert, although he hoped against hope that she would. This was not to happen, but when Robert remarried in 1578, Elizabeth was furious, and although she welcomed him back at court after a brief period of banishment, she never forgave his wife, calling her "that She-Wolf".[44]

In 1601, two years before she died, Elizabeth "had reached a state of physical and mental collapse".[45] Her mental state bordered on paranoia, and the old Queen kept a rusty sword on her table to defend herself from would-be attackers. She often thrust this sword into the arras, ensuring there were no assassins hiding behind it. She was also severely depressed. In her youth, she loved finery and beautiful clothes, but now she was dishevelled and unkempt, wearing the same dress for days. The Queen's "craziness" was well-known in court circles.[46]

It was Elizabeth's greatest fear that if she nominated a successor, courtiers would gather around him or her, and she preferred to remain the centre of attention. In 1566, the French ambassador observed that Elizabeth "had no desire to be buried alive, like her sister". The memory of droves of scheming courtiers leaving Mary's deathbed and hurrying to pay their respects to her successor must have made an indelible mark on Elizabeth since at the end of her life she often repeated the Latin phrase *mortua sed non sepulta*— dead but not yet buried. This was Elizabeth's response to the "many rumours" concerning her death in 1599.[47]

As Elizabeth aged, the question of who would succeed England's Virgin Queen was asked more frequently than ever. King James VI of Scotland, son of the executed Mary Queen of Scots, was the most likely successor. Elizabeth's courtiers "adored him as the rising sun, and neglected her as being now ready to set".[48] Just like her sister, Elizabeth was buried alive by her fickle courtiers, who were now weary of the Virgin Queen's longevity and flocked to James's side.

Queen Elizabeth died on 24 March 1603. She outlived her sister Mary by forty-five years and died as an old woman. In her final illness, Elizabeth refused to take to bed, eat or accept medical help. When the Lord Admiral

Charles Howard, her kinsman, was summoned to the Queen's side, he encouraged her to rest in bed instead of sitting motionlessly on the floor among her cushions with a finger constantly in her mouth. It was believed that he would be able to persuade the Queen to rest, but Elizabeth "said softly to him if he had known what she had seen in her bed he would not persuade her as he did".[49] The Lord Admiral had at least managed to convince Elizabeth to eat some broth, but the Queen complained that she felt as if "tied with a chain of iron about my neck". Two of her ladies discovered a queen of hearts playing card "with an iron nail knocked through the head of it" underneath Elizabeth's chair. The ladies were afraid to remove the card, "thinking it to be some witchcraft".[50] In reality, it was not witchcraft that killed Elizabeth; the Queen was troubled with a "sore throat" as well as "heat in her breasts and dryness in her mouth and tongue" caused by a combination of tonsillitis and flu.[51]

Elizabeth was buried at Westminster Abbey in the crypt beneath the altar, in the sepulchre of her illustrious grandfather, to whom she bore physical resemblance, Henry VII. Three years later her coffin was placed on top of that of her sister, Mary. Today, they lay buried together beneath a monument representing Elizabeth in her coronation robes, erected by James I. There was no effigy of Mary, the only acknowledgement of her presence there being the Latin inscription: Regno consortes et urna, hic obdor mimus Elizabetha et Maria sorores, in spe resurrectionis [Partners both in throne and grave, here rest we two sisters Elizabeth and Mary, in the hope of one resurrection]. Thus the sisters who hated each other in life were consigned to spend eternity in one grave.

NOTES

[1] Steven W. May (ed.), *Queen Elizabeth I: Selected Works*, p. 34.
[2] *Calendar of State Papers, Spain (Simancas)*, Volume 1, 1558-1567, n. 1.
[3] Louis Montrose, *The Subject of Elizabeth: Authority, Gender, and Representation*, p. 38.
[4] David Loades, *Mary Tudor*, p. 371.
[5] Anna Whitelock, *Mary Tudor*, p. 305.
[6] *Calendar of State Papers, Spain (Simancas)*, Volume 1, *1558-1567*, 14 December 1558.
Charles Wriothesley, *Wriothesley's Chronicle*, Volume 2, p. 142.
[7] Hannah Leah Crummé, *Jane Dormer's Recipe for Politics*, p. 57.
[8] Sylvia Barbara Soberton, *Great Ladies*, pp. 214-215.
[9] *Calendar of State Papers, Venice*, Volume 7, n. 10.
[10] Janet Arnold, *Queen Elizabeth's Wardrobe Unlock'd*, pp. 254-255.
[11] *Calendar of State Papers, Venice*, Volume 7, n. 10.
[12] Agnes Strickland, *Lives of the Queens of England*, p. 352.
[13] S. Duncan, *Mary I: Gender, Power, and Ceremony in the Reign of England's First Queen*, p. 212.
[14] Catherine Loomis, *The Death of Elizabeth I: Remembering and Reconstructing the Virgin Queen*, p. 11.
[15] David Loades, *Mary Tudor*, p. 335.
[16] Roy Strong, *Gloriana: The Portraits of Queen Elizabeth I*, p.53.
[17] Sylvia Barbara Soberton, *Great Ladies*, p. 247.
[18] *Calendar of State Papers, Venice*, Volume 6, 1555-1558, n. 884.
[19] *Calendar of State Papers, Spain*, Volume 13, 1554-1558., n. 502.

20 Geoffrey Parker, *Imprudent King: A New Life of Philip II*, pp. 58-59.
21 *Calendar of State Papers, Spain (Simancas)*, Volume 1, n. 4.
22 Maria Perry, *The Word of a Prince*, p. 100.
23 Felix Pryor (ed.), *Elizabeth I: Her Life in Letters*, p. 43.
24 *Calendar of State Papers, Spain (Simancas)*, Volume 3, n. 189.
25 *Calendar of State Papers, Spain (Simancas)*, Volume 1, *1558-1567*, n. 122.
26 Tracy Borman, *Elizabeth's Women: The Hidden Story of the Virgin Queen*, p. 209.
27 L'anomalie hormonale d'Elisabeth Ire d'Angleterre
28 Frederick Chamberlin, *The Private Character of Queen Elizabeth*, p. 62.
29 Ibid., p. 60.
30 Ibid., p. 67.
31 Edward Jorden, *A Briefe Discourse of a Disease Called the Suffocation of the Mother*, p. 17.
32 Frederick Chamberlin, *The Private Character of Queen Elizabeth*, p. 58.
33 Susan Doran, *Monarchy and Matrimony: The Courtships of Elizabeth I*, p. 197.
34 Elizabeth Lane Furdell, *The Royal Doctors, 1485-1714*, p. 144.
35 *Letters and Papers, Foreign and Domestic, Henry VIII*, Volume 13 Part 1, n. 56.
36 Anna Whitelock, *Mary Tudor*, p. 307.
37 Margaret Aston, *The King's Bedpost: Reformation and Iconography in a Tudor Group Portrait*, p. 128.
38 Hastings Robinson, *Original Letters Relative to the English Reformation*, Volume 1, p. 343.
39 Nicola Tallis, *Elizabeth's Rival: The Tumultuous Tale of Lettice Knollys, Countess of Leicester*, p. 44.
40 Henry Clifford, *The Life of Jane Dormer, Duchess of Feria*, p. 87.
41 Elizabeth Norton, *The Temptation of Elizabeth Tudor: Elizabeth I, Thomas Seymour, and the Making of a Virgin Queen*, p. 120.
42 *Calendar of State Papers, Spain (Simancas)*, Volume 1, *1558-1567*, n. 27.
43 *Calendar of State Papers, Spain (Simancas)*, Volume 1, n. 270.
44 Ibid., Volume 3, n. 343.
45 Leanda de Lisle, *After Elizabeth*, p. 55.
46 Frederick Chamberlin, *The Private Character of Queen Elizabeth*, p. 72.

[47] Scott L. Newstok, *Quoting Death in Early Modern England: The Poetics of Epitaphs Beyond the Tomb*, p. 74.
[48] William Camden, *The History of the Most Renowned and Victorious Princess Elizabeth*, p. 659.
[49] Henry Clifford, *The Life of Jane Dormer, Duchess of Feria*, p. 99.
[50] Ibid.
[51] Frederick Chamberlin, *The Private Character of Queen Elizabeth*, p. 75.

In her book *After Elizabeth: The Rise of James of Scotland and the Struggle for the Throne of England* (p. 55), historian Leanda de Lisle suggested that the Queen suffered from Ludwig's angina.

Picture Section

Figure 1: Katharine of Aragon, mother of Mary Tudor.

Figure 2: Anne Boleyn, Elizabeth's mother.

Picture section

Figure 3: The Family Portrait of Henry VIII c. 1545, symbolising succession to the throne.

Figure 4: Mary, aged twenty-nine, as depicted in The Family Portrait of Henry VIII.

Figure 5: Elizabeth, aged twelve, as depicted in The Family Portrait of Henry VIII.

Picture section

Figure 6: Mary in 1544, ages twenty-eight. "Her beauty is mediocre, and it may be said that she is one of the belles of this Court", wrote the French ambassador.

Figure 7: Elizabeth as a teenager during the reign of her half brother Edward VI. "For the face, I grant, I might well blush to offer, but the mind I shall never be ashamed to present", she wrote in a letter accompanying this portrait.

Picture section

Figure 8: Edward VI c. 1552. His last will known as 'my devise for succession' almost deprived Mary and Elizabeth of their royal inheritance.

Figure 9: Mary Tudor as Queen of England, c. 1554.

Figure 10: Philip II of Spain, Mary's husband.

Figure 11: Coronation portrait of Queen Elizabeth, 1558.

Selected Bibliography

Printed primary sources

Ascham, R. *The Whole Works of Roger Ascham.* John Russel Smith, 1865.

Bietenholz, P.G. *The Correspondence of Erasmus: Letters 842-992 (1518-1519).* University of Toronto Press, 1982.

Blatcher, M. *Seymour Papers 1532-1686.* H.M.S.O, 1968.

Brewer, J.S. & Gairdner, J., eds. *Calendar of State Papers, Spain.* Institute of Historical Research (1862-1932).

Brewer, J.S. & Gairdner, J., eds. *Letters and Papers, Foreign and Domestic, of the Reign of Henry VIII.* 28 Volumes. Institute of Historical Research (1862-1932).

Brigden, S. ed. *The Letters of Richard Scudamore to Sir Philip Hoby, September 1549-March 1555.* Camden Miscellany, xxx, (Camden Soc. 4th ser. 39, 1990).

Camden, W. *The History of the Most Renowned and Victorious Princess Elizabeth Late Queen of England.* Flesher, 1688.

Clifford, H. *The Life of Jane Dormer, Duchess of Feria.* Burns & Oates, 1887.

Dowling, M., ed. *William Latymer's Cronickille of Anne Bulleyne.* Camden Miscellany, xxx (Camden Soc. 4th ser. 39, 1990).

Ellis, H. *Original Letters Illustrative of English History*, Volume 2. (2nd series). Harding and Lepard, 1827.

Everett Wood, A. *Letters of Royal and Illustrious Ladies of Great Britain, Three Volumes.* London: H. Colburn, 1846.

Foxe, J. *The Actes and Monuments of the Church.* Hobart Seymour, ed. M. Robert Carter & Brothers, 1855.

Gough Nichols, J. *The Chronicle of Queen Jane and of Two Years of Queen Mary.* Camden Society, 1850.

Gough Nichols, J. *The Literary Remains of Edward the Sixth. Edited From His Autograph Manuscripts, With Historical Notes and a Biographical Memoir.* J.B. Nichols, 1859.

Hall, E. *Hall's Chronicle.* J. Johnson, 1809.

Harris, N. *The Literary Remains of Lady Jane Grey: With a Memoir of Her Life.* Harding, Triphook, and Lepard, 1825.

Haynes, S. *A Collection of State Papers: relating to Affairs In the Reigns of King Henry VIII, King Edward VI, Queen Mary and Queen Elizabeth: From the Year 1542 to 1570.* Bowyer, 1740.

Leland, J. *Joannis Lelandi antiquarii de rebus britannicis collectanea.* Richardson, 1770.

Madden, F. *Privy Purse Expenses of the Princess Mary, Daughter of King Henry the Eighth, Afterwards Queen Mary: With a Memoir of the Princess, and Notes.* William Pickering, 1831.

Mueller, J., ed. *Katherine Parr: Complete Works and Correspondence.* University of Chicago Press, 2011.

Sander, N. *Rise and Growth of the Anglican Schism.* Burns and Oates, 1877.

Sharp Hume, M.A. *Chronicle of King Henry VIII of England.* George Bell and Sons, 1889.

St Clare Byrne, M., ed. *The Lisle Letters.* Six Volumes. The University of Chicago Press, 1981.

Wriothesley, C. *A Chronicle of England During the Reigns of the Tudors, from A.D. 1485 to 1559.* Two Volumes. Camden Society, 1875.

Selected Bibliography

Secondary sources

Arnold, J. *Queen Elizabeth's Wardrobe Unlock'd.* Maney Publishing, 1988.

Bernard, G.W. *Anne Boleyn: Fatal Attractions.* Yale University Press, 2010.

Bernard, G.W. *The King's Reformation.* Yale University Press, 2007.

Borman, T. *Elizabeth's Women: The Hidden Story of the Virgin Queen.* Vintage, 2010.

Borman, T. *The Private Lives of the Tudors: Uncovering the Secrets of Britain's Greatest Dynasty.* Hodder & Stoughton, 2016.

Chamberlin, F. *The Private Character of Queen Elizabeth.* Dodd Mead & Company, 1922.

Childs, J. *Henry VIII's Last Victim: The Life and Times of Henry Howard, Earl of Surrey.* Thomas Dunne Books, 2007.

Collins, A. *Letters and Memorials of State.* Volume 2. T. Osborne, 1746.

Doran, S. *Elizabeth I and Her Circle.* Oxford University Press, 2015.

Erickson, C. *The First Elizabeth.* Macmillan, 2007.

Evans, V.S. *Ladies-in-Waiting: Women Who Served at the Tudor Court.* CreateSpace, 2014.

Fox, J. *Jane Boleyn: The True Story of the Infamous Lady Rochford.* Ballantine Books, 2009.

Fraser Tytler, P. *England under the Reigns of Edward VI and Mary.* Richard Bentley, 1839.

Friedmann, P. *Anne Boleyn: A Chapter of English History, 1527-1536.* Macmillan and Co., 1884.

Furdel Lane, E. *The Royal Doctors, 1485-1714: Medical Personnel at the Tudor and Stuart Courts.* University of Rochester Press, 2001.

Gladish, D.M. *The Tudor Privy Council.* Redford, 1915.

Hamilton, D.B. *Shakespeare and the Politics of Protestant England.* University Press of Kentucky, 1992.

Harkrider, F.M. *Women, Reform and Community in Early Modern England.* Boydell Press, 2008.

Harris, J.B. *English Aristocratic Women, 1450-1550: Marriage and Family, Property and Careers.* Oxford University Press, 2002.

Head, M.D. *The Ebbs and Flows of Fortune: The Life of Thomas Howard, Third Duke of Norfolk.* University of Georgia Press, 1995.

Hibbert, C. *The Virgin Queen: A Personal History of Elizabeth I.* Tauris Parke Paperbacks, 2010.

Hutchinson, R. *The Last Days of Henry VIII: Conspiracy, Treason and Heresy at the Court of the Dying Tyrant.* Phoenix, 2006.

Ives, E. W. *The Life and Death of Anne Boleyn: The Most Happy.* Blackwell Publishing, 2010.

James, S. *Catherine Parr: Henry VIII's Last Love.* The History Press, 2010.

Kelly, H.A. *The Matrimonial Trials of Henry VIII.* Wipf and Stock Publishers, 2004.

Klarwill, V. *Queen Elizabeth and Some Foreigners.* Bentano's, 1928.

Lipscomb, S. *1536: The Year that Changed Henry VIII.* Lion Hudson, 2009.

Loades, D. *Mary Tudor: A Life.* Basil Blackwell, 1989.

Loomis, C. "Elizabeth Southwell's Manuscript Account of the Death of Queen Elizabeth [with Text]". *English Literary Renaissance*, Vol. 26, No. 3, Monarchs (1996), pp. 482-509.

Selected Bibliography

Merriman, R.B. *Life and Letters of Thomas Cromwell*. Two Volumes. Clarendon Press, 1902.

Montrose, L. *The Subject of Elizabeth: Authority, Gender, and Representation*. University of Chicago Press, 2006.

Myers, A.R. *The Household of Edward IV*. Manchester University Press, 1959.

North, J. *England's Boy King: The Diary of Edward VI, 1547-1553*. Ravenhall, 2005.

Norton, E. *Anne of Cleves: Henry VIII's Discarded Bride*. Amberley Publishing, 2011.

Norton, E. *Bessie Blount: Mistress to Henry VIII*. Amberley Publishing, 2012.

Norton, E. *Jane Seymour: Henry VIII's True Love*. Amberley Publishing, 2010.

Norton, E. *The Boleyn Women: The Tudor Femmes Fatales Who Changed English History*. Amberley Publishing, 2013.

Porter, L. *Katherine the Queen: The Remarkable Life of Katherine Parr*. Macmillan, 2010.

Riehl, A. *The Face of Queenship: Early Modern Representations of Elizabeth I*. Palgrave Macmillan, 2010.

Scarisbrick, J.J. *Henry VIII*. University of California Press, 1968.

Schofield, J. *The Rise and Fall of Thomas Cromwell: Henry VIII's Most Faithful Servant*. The History Press, 2011.

Smith, Lacey B. *Catherine Howard: The Queen Whose Adulteries Made a Fool of Henry VIII*. Amberley Publishing, 2009.

Soberton, S.B. *Great Ladies: The Forgotten Witnesses to the Lives of Tudor Queens*. CreateSpace, 2017.

Starkey, D. *Elizabeth: The Struggle for the Throne.* Harper Perennial, 2007.

Starkey, D. *Six Wives: The Queens of Henry VIII.* Vintage, 2004.

Stone, J.M. *History of Mary I, Queen of England.* Sands & Co., 1901.

Strong, R. *Artists of the Tudor Court.* Victoria & Albert Museum, 1983.

Tremlett, G. *Catherine of Aragon: Henry's Spanish Queen.* Faber & Faber, 2010.

Varlow, S. "Sir Francis Knollys's Latin Dictionary: New Evidence for Katherine Carey". *Historical Research*, 80 (2007), 315-23.

Walker, G. "Rethinking the Fall of Anne Boleyn". *The Historical Journal*, Vol. 45, No. 1 (Mar., 2002), pp. 1-29.

Warnicke, R.M. *The Rise and Fall of Anne Boleyn: Family Politics at the Court of Henry VIII.* Cambridge University Press, 1991.

Warnicke, R.M. *Wicked Women of Tudor England.* Palgrave MacMillan, 2012.

Weir, A. *Elizabeth of York: A Tudor Queen and Her World.* Ballantine Books, 2013.

Weir, A. *Mary Boleyn: "The Great and Infamous Whore".* Vintage, 2011.

Weir, A. *The Lady in the Tower: The Fall of Anne Boleyn.* Vintage, 2010.

Weir, A. *The Six Wives of Henry VIII.* Vintage, 2007.

Whitelock, A. *Elizabeth's Bedfellows: An Intimate History of the Queen's Court.* Bloomsbury Publishing, 2013.

Whitelock, A. *Mary Tudor: England's First Queen.* Bloomsbury Publishing, 2010.

Whitelock, A. *Tudor Queenship: The Reigns of Mary and Elizabeth*. Palgrave Macmillan, 2012.

Wilkinson, J. *Katherine Howard: The Tragic Story of Henry VIII's Fifth Queen*. Hachette UK, 2016.

Williams, P. *Catherine of Aragon: The Tragic Story of Henry VIII's First Unfortunate Wife*. Amberley Publishing, 2013.

Wilson, A. V. *Queen Elizabeth's Maids of Honour and Ladies of the Privy Chamber*. John Lane, 1922.

Made in the USA
Columbia, SC
16 July 2021